Withdrawn

ACC NO. 3878

01

D1146477

Investigating Textiles

Margaret Gamble

HODDER AND STOUGHTON

LONDON SYDNEY AUCKLAND TORONTO

Acknowledgments

I should like to thank Mary Roberts for allowing me to include her Suffolk Puff Box; Mr N A Roberts for the photography, and, of course all my long-suffering students for working through my initial ideas, firstly in College, and then in schools.

My gratitude also goes to my family for their constant encouragement and support during the writing of this book.

746 .

Margaret Gamble
Senior Lecturer in Fashion & Textiles
North East Worcestershire College
Bromsgove

1988

© 1989 Margaret Gamble

First published in Great Britain 1989
Second impression 1989

ISBN 0 340 48529 9

All rights reserved. No part of this publication may be reproduced or transmitted in any form or by any means, electronically or mechanically, including photocopying, recording or any information storage or retrieval system, without either the prior permission in writing from the publisher or a licence permitting restricted copying. In the United Kingdom such licences are issued by the Copyright Licensing Agency, 33–34 Alfred Place, London WC1E 7DP

Typeset in Linotron Optima by Rowland Phototypesetting Limited, Bury St Edmunds, Suffolk
Printed and bound in Great Britain for Edward Arnold, the educational, academic and medical publishing division of Hodder and Stoughton Limited, Mill Road, Dunton Green, Sevenoaks, Kent by St Edmundsbury Press Limited, Bury St Edmunds, Suffolk

Contents

Introduction

This teacher's book has been written to encourage the development of creative ideas from both teacher and pupil who together are working within an examination structure.

The book consists of 25 ideas that may be used as part of a programme for coursework for GCSE Textiles. The ideas can be complete small projects or they can form the basis for samples for future projects.

These ideas give the pupil the opportunity to use and thereby develop the prescribed investigation, measurement, communication, management, psycho-motor and technological skills, whilst learning practical textile skills and techniques.

The ideas are graded according to the age and ability of the pupil, and they are designed to be completed in a set time. Each idea is also set out so that any prerequisite knowledge is identified, as are any new learning activities and assessment criteria.

The book should be used as a resource rather than a set of ideas to be repeated. The ideas themselves are interchangeable and may be combined: if, for example, the teacher wishes to teach the practical skill of marbling (Marbled Patterns—Project 10), but wishes also to include another technique such as lacing and padding (Spray-Dyed Padded Frames—Project 11), then a marbled padded frame could be made. Similarly fabrics may be marbled for the Suffolk Puff Box (Project 19) to combine the technique with an introduction to patchwork techniques.

Each idea provides an introduction to further project work, which can be design or investigation based, therefore giving the pupil a taste of the techniques involved in a particular area of textiles, and providing an opportunity for the choice of further research.

The illustrations for each idea are presented in notebook form with appropriate notes, hints and possible problems. This style of presentation also serves as an example of how to keep a record of work. This follows the requirements of GCSE—a record of work which includes noting any problems encountered and how they were resolved. The 'Hints' are seen as the 'evaluation' of the idea—e.g. how the work could be improved next time; in other words the results of the investigation.

The book sets out to give the teacher an opportunity to assess continually the ideas for classwork by referring to the assessment criteria. Such criteria may be broken down and placed in a set marking grid to suit the differing needs of various examination boards.

The final chapter brings together some of the coursework into one major project which is used as a working example. This takes the form of a hypothetical, teacher-set brief and includes some detailed guidelines on how the brief might be answered, together with a list of hints for classroom management.

1   **Food advertising**

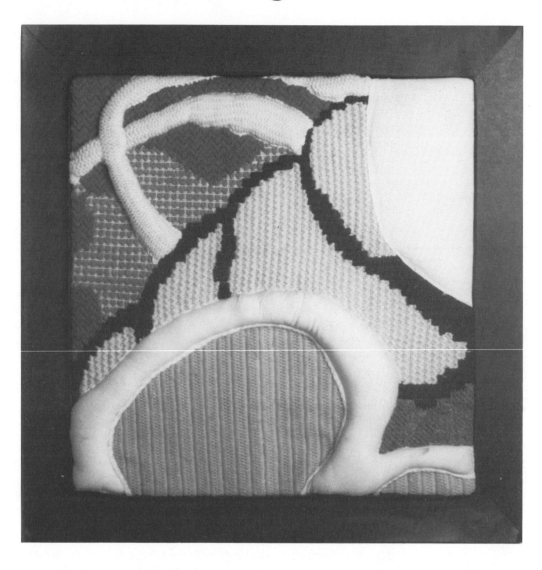

Materials and Equipment	Pencil, ruler, eraser, graph paper, tracing paper.
Approximate Time	1 hour (design only).
Age Group/Ability	13 to 16 years. Average ability. (Age group and ability according to design chosen.)
Prerequisite Knowledge	None for initial design.
Learning Activities	• To forge an introductory link between food and textile design. • Scaling-up part of a design. • Recognition of shape and colour as a basis for good design. • Interpreting an original design into embroidery methods.
Assessment Criteria	• The ability to recognise and select an area to extend into a design. • The ability to alter the design to meet the needs of the task involved. • The ability to translate the design into suitable embroidery methods.
Development of the Project	As shown in the interpretation, the design may be translated into various creative methods as a main project for assessment: e.g. woollen yarns used for the canvas work were dyed using vegetable dyes; experimentation with knitting and canvas stitches, appliqué. Other translations of the design: soft sculpture.

HINTS:
1. The right angled paper strips can be used for any size of design.
2. The advert chosen must have clear bold shapes for ease of scaling up.
3. The scaling can be speeded up by the use of ruled and squared centimetre paper.

PROBLEMS:
The scaling must be accurate otherwise the design becomes distorted.

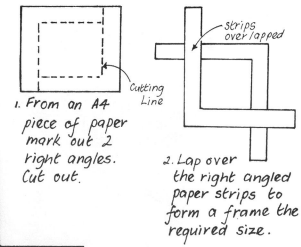

1. From an A4 piece of paper mark out 2 right angles. Cut out.

2. Lap over the right angled paper strips to form a frame the required size.

3. Choose an advert from a magazine. Select an area which has clear lines, bold shapes, and interesting colour combination.

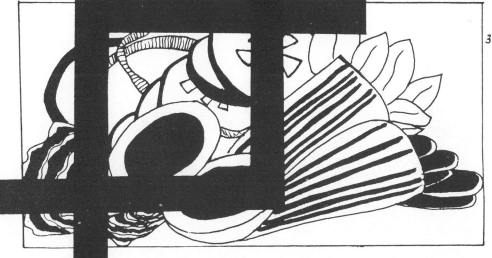

4. Trace off the outlines of the selected area. Divide into 0.5 cm squares.
Adapt design
e.g. ---- = lines deleted.

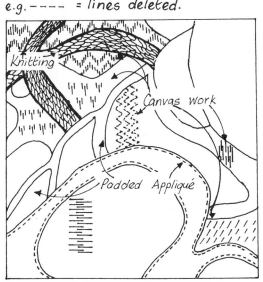

Knitting

Canvas work

Padded Appliqué

5. Scale up to DOUBLE the original size by using 1cm squared paper. Draw one square at a time, starting at 1A.

6. Experiment with textile techniques to translate the design.
e.g. The combined use of threads, yarns, fabrics in Appliqué, Canvas work and Knitting.

2 Botanical design

Materials and Equipment	Botany books, gardening magazines and books, paper for drawing, tracing paper, pencil, eraser.
Approximate Time	1 hour.
Age Group/Ability	13 years upwards.
Prerequisite Knowledge	None.
Learning Activities	• To enable the pupils to be aware of the world about them, and to see that designs for textiles may be taken from everyday things. • To encourage original design work. • To encourage an aesthetic appreciation of design, and its application to textiles. • Decision making.
Assessment Criteria	• The selection of initial drawings or pictures, and how they have been adapted. • The approach to design, and the decision making that has taken place. • The final design, and how it may be used in the various aspects of textiles.
Development of the Project	Carrying the design ideas through to interpretation in a textile form. Evaluating the result.

HINTS:

1. It is advisable to choose diagrams that are similar in shape so that they will easily combine.
2. Parts of the diagrams can be scaled up or down to achieve a more interesting design.

PROBLEMS:

If the biological drawings chosen are complicated, the outline shapes of the diagrams only should be used.

Diagram A.

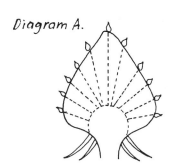

L.S. of Strawberry

Diagram B.

L.S. of Buttercup

1. Select two diagrams. Trace out each diagram.

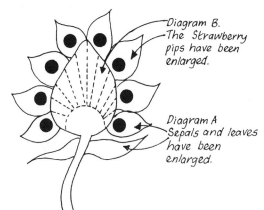

Diagram B. The Strawberry pips have been enlarged.

Diagram A Sepals and leaves have been enlarged.

2. Experiment by placing one tracing on top of the other. Combine the two drawings by selecting some of the shapes from each.

 lines altered.

3. Adapt the design by altering the original lines of the drawing and adding further lines inside the drawing.

4. The final design shown as a single screen print.

Ideas: Single design as a motif for embroidery and clothing.

Double design for a wall hanging or other home furnishings.

Several designs used for a border pattern.

3   Scrunch design

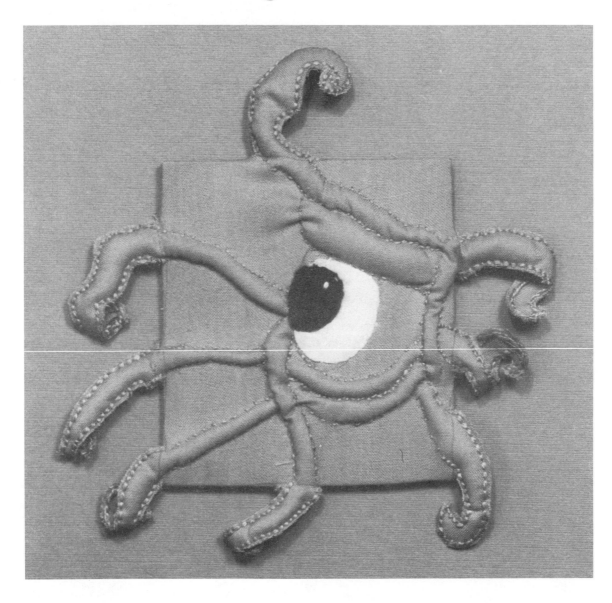

Materials and Equipment	Plain paper which retains its creases when scrunched, soft lead pencil, eraser, coloured paper for frame, tracing paper.
Approximate Time	1 hour.
Age Group/Ability	11 years upwards. Average ability.
Prerequisite Knowledge	None.
Learning Activities	• To give the pupil confidence in producing an original design. • Isolating a design area and translating it into a textile technique. • To encourage the pupil to use his or her imagination, and to appreciate the importance of design in textile work.
Assessment Criteria	• A methodical procedure in carrying out the task. • The selection of isolated areas. • The interpretation of the isolated areas into textile form.
Development of the Project	Using one or more of the designs in a textile project, e.g. soft sculpture, Octopus.

HINTS:

1. The paper must be 'scrunched' tightly.
2. A soft lead pencil gives the best result when shading.

PROBLEMS:

The 'scrunch' lines do not always suggest a design within themselves. The work should be looked at again through half closed eyes. The addition or deletion of lines will also help.

1. 'Scrunch' up a sheet of paper. Shade across the paper using a lead pencil.

2. Place the 'scrunched' paper R.S. down on to the second sheet of paper. Rub the w.s. of the 'scrunched' paper with the edge of a ruler until the crease lines have been transferred.

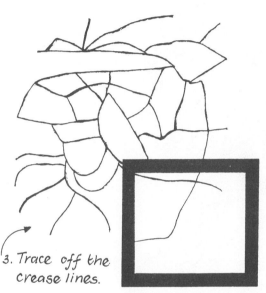

3. Trace off the crease lines.

4. Cut a small paper frame.

Design A

5. Using the paper frame move it around the drawn crease lines to select a design.

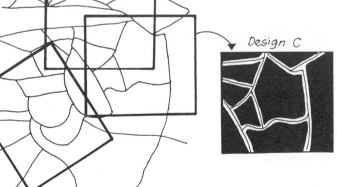

Design C

Design B

6. Adapt and colour in the design.

Ideas:-

Design A

A landscape or aerial view which can be embroidered.

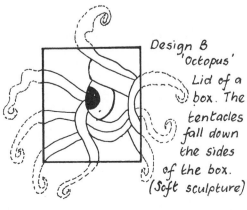

Design B
'Octopus'
Lid of a box. The tentacles fall down the sides of the box. (Soft sculpture)

Design C

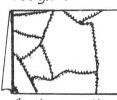

Audio cassette case worked in crazy patchwork using fabrics/leather.

4 Computer faces

Materials and Equipment	Design Sources (magazines, newspapers, catalogues, etc.), pencil, ruler, eraser, coloured pencils or felt-tip pens, graph paper, tracing paper. A computer could be used.
Approximate Time	1 hour, if an illustration has already been selected.
Age Group/Ability	13 years upwards. Average ability.
Prerequisite Knowledge	Understanding of good design. The colour wheel.
Learning Activities	• Selecting material for design work. • Appreciating line, shape, and form. • Drawing, modifying, and translating a design. • Using imagination throughout the task to present an original piece of work.
Assessment Criteria	• Decision making—selection of the initial illustration. • Translation of the illustration into tonal areas. • The ability to adapt a design into a pattern for imaginative interpretation using various textile techniques.
Development of the Project	Using the completed design for interpretation in any aspect of textiles.

HINTS:

1. A face with distinctive features should be chosen as a source for design.
2. It is essential that the completed design does not resemble the original ~ the imagination must be used.

PROBLEM:

It may be difficult to reduce the chosen design into only 3 tonal areas. If this is the case, try squinting at the original design source.

1. Trace the outline, features, and shading from a face.

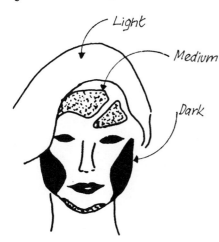

Light

Medium

Dark

2. Delete some of the lines on the face - simplifying the design, e.g. eyebrows, crease lines, earrings etc. Select the areas to be coloured into DARK, MEDIUM, and LIGHT tones.

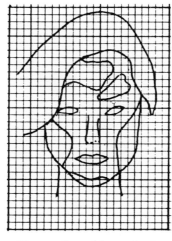

3. Transfer the design (by tracing off) on to graph paper.

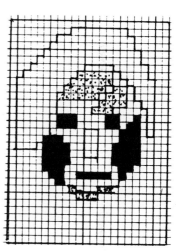

4. Using the graph paper as a guideline block in the design using the chosen colour tones.

Ideas for translation:-

a.) KNITWEAR - (1 square = 1 stitch)

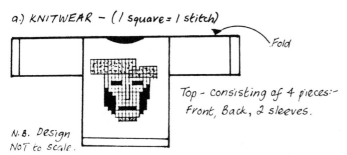

Fold

Top - consisting of 4 pieces:- Front, Back, 2 sleeves.

N.B. Design NOT to scale.

b.) 3-D EMBROIDERY - "The Boxer" (Adaptation shown in photograph)

Using Appliqué, Canvas work, Machine embroidery, Leather work together with some Craft techniques.

c.) POSTER - Using paints, and fabric dyes, or translated into Batik.

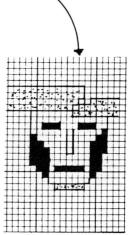

5. OPTIONAL:- Adapt the design further if required.

5 Magazine jigsaws

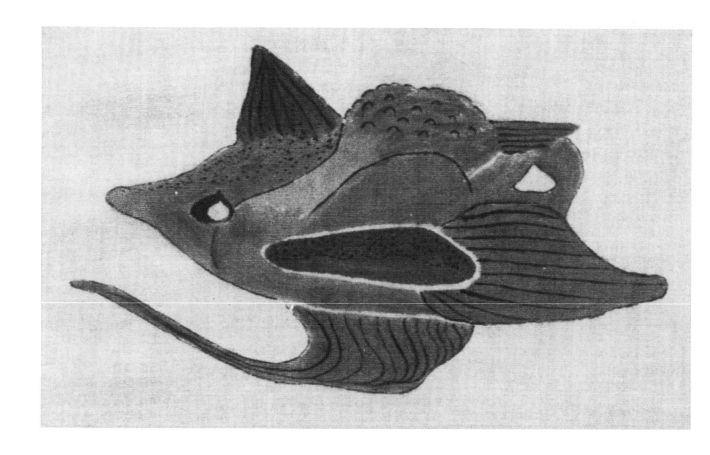

Materials and Equipment	Magazine pictures, pencils, paper, scissors, adhesive.
Approximate Time	1 hour.
Age Group/Ability	13 years upwards. Above average ability.
Prerequisite Knowledge	Experience of shape and colour.
Learning Activities	• Experimental and investigatory work with colour, line, shape, texture, and composition, including scaling up a design. • Evaluating the completed design, and considering its use in relation to textiles.
Assessment Criteria	• An appreciation of the importance of good design. • The choice of original drawing and its interpretation. • The skilful use of tools and materials. • Decisions and choices made in relation to the task.
Development of the Project	• Design and its importance in the enhancement of the home, including different ways that design influences the home environment. • Design used as a clothing decoration, and for surface pattern on fabrics. • The effect of design on our everyday lives, e.g. consumerism.

HINTS:
1. The original drawing must have clear outlines.
2. The design shapes should be cut out accurately to obtain a good result.
3. Choose various shapes within the drawing e.g. curved, angular etc.

PROBLEMS:
The cut pieces of the design may not readily form a recognisable image. In this case an abstract pattern may result which can also be used.

1. Original drawing.

2. Outline traced and divided into squares.

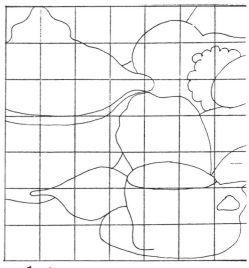

3. Scaling up.
   N.B. Scaling is optional. The drawing may be used its original size.

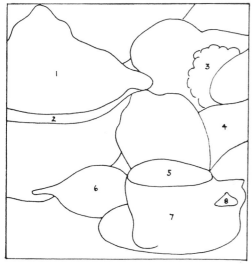

4. Divide drawing into sections and number, by selecting shapes.

5. Cut out the numbered shapes.

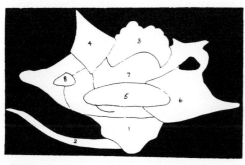

6. Experiment with the shapes by moving them around within a frame HALF the size of the original drawing. The shapes may be turned over, inverted, overlapped.

7. Trace off the design.

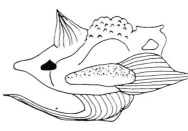

8. Add details. The design may be used for embroidery, motif for clothing, or household decoration.

Ideas: Jeans badge

15

6 Folded landscapes

Materials and Equipment	Any lightweight fabric e.g. cotton polyester, muslin, silk, Vilene etc., selection of embroidery threads, needle, pins, ruler, pencil, craft knife, iron and ironing board, cardboard, sellotape, fabric paints or dyes, plain paper, paint brushes, mixing palette.
Approximate Time	2 to 2½ hours.
Age Group/Ability	13 to 14 years. Average ability range.
Prerequisite Knowledge	• Cutting a mount. • A basic understanding of colour and embroidery stitches.
Learning Activities	• An introduction to the use and behaviour of dyes on fabric, together with the manipulation of fabrics. • The use and extension of basic embroidery stitches. • The mounting and presentation of work, including keeping a diary of the task.
Assessment Criteria	• The application and appreciation of colour. • An awareness of the reaction of dyes on fabrics. • The selection and experimentation of fabric into a 3-D form. • The imaginative interpretation of the task at all stages, and pupil's record of the work. • The skilful and accurate use of tools. • The presentation of the finished work.
Development of the Project	It provides a starting point for investigation into dyes and their reaction to various fabrics. This can be extended to the choice of fabrics for clothing and the home. The manipulation of fabrics leads to an investigation of the properties and handling qualities of fabric suitable for the purpose in mind. NB This project also leads into the next experimental project 'Fabric-Strip Weaving'.

HINTS:
1. The size 14cm x 9cm is most practical.
2. To produce the most effective landscape patterns use a series of colours in progressive tones.
3. To speed up the drying process a hairdryer may be used, or the fabric can be ironed between paper. The ironing method produces very subtle colouring.
4. The paint or dye must be well watered for the colours to run into each other.

PROBLEMS:
It is advisable to try out the dyes on spare fabric first.

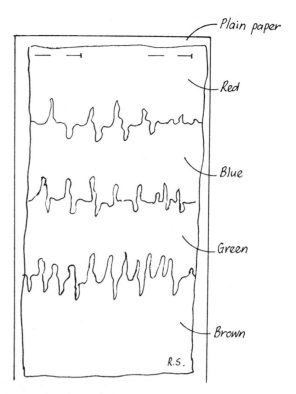

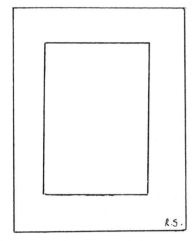

1. Cut a cardboard frame to fit the size of the required finished work. Press the fabric to remove all creases.

2. Place the fabric on a piece of plain paper and pin. With a SOFT paint brush apply the watered down dye. The dye is applied in bands of colour so that they merge, giving different effects according to the amount of dye and type of fabric being used.

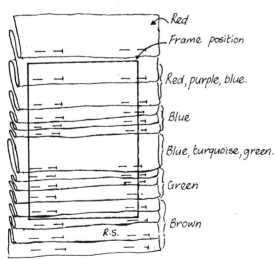

3. Allow the fabric to dry on the paper. Set the dye by ironing. Using pins at the side of the work, fold the fabric horizontally, vertically or diagonally to produce the desired effect. Hold the cardboard frame over the folded fabric, until an interesting landscape is produced.

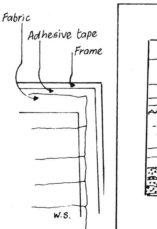
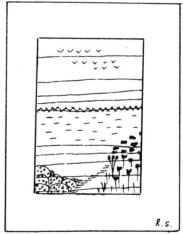

4. Re-position the pins to WITHIN the frame, and trim the fabric edges to correspond with the frame.
Remove the frame, and trim the fabric edges another 0.5cm Using clear adhesive tape, attach the w.s. of the fabric to the w.s. of the frame. This forms a basis for working the embroidery.

7   Fabric-strip weaving

Materials and Equipment	Fabric remnants from 'Folded Landscapes' and the cardboard remaining from the mount used, or cardboard measuring 9 cm × 6 cm, craft knife, pencil, ruler, sellotape, scissors, fine thread for warp. NB Any lightweight fabric may be used, in place of remnants from the previous project.
Approximate Time	1 hour.
Age Group/Ability	12 to 14 years. Average ability range.
Prerequisite Knowledge	'Folded Landscapes' project or a knowledge of painting fabric with dyes to give and create an interesting effect.
Learning Activities	• The basic principles of weaving, together with using a more imaginative and original approach. • An aesthetic appreciation of texture and colour, together with its application to clothing and the home. • Experimentation with and investigation into various textural effects. • Creating a textural piece, and in doing so recording the problems involved, together with the results.
Assessment Criteria	• The application and appreciation of texture and colour. • Manipulative skills—tearing fabric, making a card loom, weaving. • Inventiveness and a problem solving approach to the work, including the working method. • A recognition of the relationship between texture and fabric construction.
Development of the Project	It provides a starting point for further investigation into weaving methods (and other methods of constructing fabrics), ancient weaving crafts (e.g. braid loom, finger weaving), and textural effects as a basis and inspiration for embroidery work.

HINTS:

1. The remnants of card and fabric from 'Folded Landscapes' can be used for this project. Otherwise, the loom may be any size, but small card looms are preferable.
2. To provide a simple measurement, the warp threads may be strung 1.cm. apart and the fabric strips cut or torn 1.c.m. wide.
3. Pupils can experiment with varying warp thread spacing, and varying widths of fabric strips to investigate further textural possibilities.
4. The project is an 'experimental' piece. A 'neat' effect will destroy the textural effect.

PROBLEMS:

1. Loom notches must be cut accurately.
2. Fabric strips are difficult to weave; a large eyed needle may be used.
3. Warp thread must be fine, yet strong.

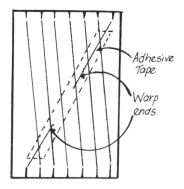

1. Cut notches at top and base of card 1.c.m. apart. Wind on the WARP thread to form a loom.

2. On the w.s. tape down the warp ends.

Adhesive Tape

Warp ends

Area used for Folded Landscape

3. Using the spare fabric divide into 1.c.m. strips by cutting or tearing.

ALTERNATIVE:

strips may be cut in varying widths to give a more interesting result.

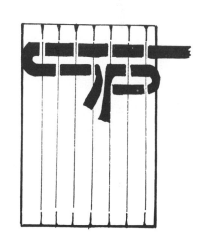

4. Ends can be tied at the front of the work to give a 'ragged' textural effect.

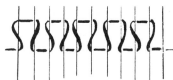

5. Further textural effects can be achieved by:-

a) Twisting fabric strips

b) Plaiting Fabric strips

c) Tying the warp threads

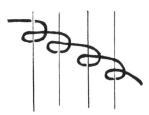

d) Wrapping strips around warp thread.

e) Twisting the strips over and under the warp thread.

8   Prints from paper

Materials and Equipment	Wrapping paper, food labels, paper bags, pencil, scissors, dry iron, ironing board, newspaper (to cover board), plain paper (to cover board), greaseproof paper or thin plain paper, a range of fabrics e.g. polyester cotton, synthetics, muslin to test printed papers.
Approximate Time	1 hour.
Age Group/Ability	11 years upwards. Low to above average ability. The work can be easily adapted for higher ability pupils.
Prerequisite Knowledge	• A previous introduction to experimentation and problem solving would be useful, but not essential. • Colour and shape recognition.
Learning Activities	• An appreciation of colour and shape. • Experimentation with fabrics, and their printing qualities. • Accurate measurement, and the estimation of fitting shape into a specific area. • Interpreting the use of paper for printing in a creative way. • The development of a knowledge of fabrics and their reaction to dyes. • Carrying out a task within a time limit.
Assessment Criteria	• The interpretation and aesthetic appreciation of colour and shape. • The ability to use measurement accurately. • The effective use of tools and materials to produce the desired result, e.g. a good, clear, print. • Experimentation and decision-making throughout the project.
Development of the Project	Further investigation into dyes and printing methods. The effects of surface pattern on fabrics in fashion and furnishings. Experimentation with other forms of printing on fabric, e.g. block, screen etc. Using paper prints as a background for embroidery e.g. quilting, canvas work, patchwork.

HINTS:

1. The most successful fabrics for printing are pure synthetics and polyester/cotton mixtures.
2. The colour of the print will vary according to a) the fabric used b) the heat of the iron; therefore the colours of the printed paper do not necessarily represent exactly the colours of the fabric print.
3. The iron must be HOT - check whether the paper is printing by pulling back a corner.

PROBLEMS:

1. Some papers do NOT print (pupils could investigate)
2. Paper bags must be opened out carefully.
3. Thin paper moves under the iron giving a blurred image.

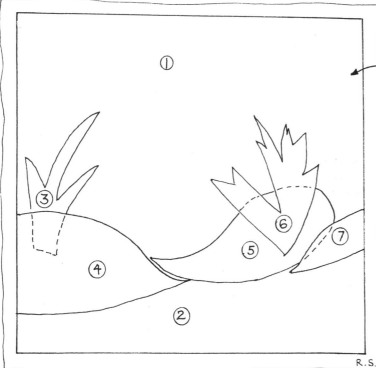

Used as a foreground ②

After experimenting:-

1. Choose 4 papers which will print well on the chosen fabric. (A,B,C,D)

2. From these 4 papers choose ONE most suitable for a 'backdrop' (Paper A) ①

3. Select shapes from the remaining papers. (B,C,D) Cut out.

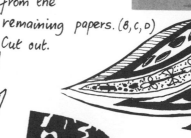

4. On plain paper (size A4) experiment with the background paper and shapes, until a pleasant design is created.

5. Glue the completed design on to the A4 paper in numerical order. N.B. An adhesive stick is most suitable as some glues cause shrivelling.

6. Place the fabric R.S. on the ironing board, and the design R.S. down. Press with a hot iron, moving it slowly across the work.

9 Doodle poly-prints

Materials and Equipment	Polystyrene tile, craft knife, pencil, card (same size as the tile), plate of glass or piece of plastic or a sheet of acetate for rolling dye, roller, block printing ink, PVA, fabric for printing, e.g. plain cotton without dressing.
Approximate Time	1½ hours.
Age Group/Ability	13 years upwards. Any ability.
Prerequisite Knowledge	None.
Learning Activities	• To learn the technique of block printing, and its versatility for textiles. • To encourage original design, and a sense of achievement. • The use of tools and equipment.
Assessment Criteria	• The choice of design in relation to the task. • The ability to use tools. • The ability to solve problems. • The production of an imaginative and skilfully printed piece of work.
Development of the Project	Development into other forms of printing fabrics, e.g. screen. Other methods of printing with blocks, e.g. lino, stamp, etc.

HINTS:

1. A blunt pencil should be used to draw on the polystyrene.
2. A very sharp craft knife should be used to cut the polystyrene to avoid it flaking.
3. Ensure the glued template is securely fixed before printing.
4. The block printing ink/paint should be the correct consistency i.e. it should drag slightly and sound 'sticky' when rolled on the glass.
5. The placing of the template requires accuracy. Mark 'top' and 'base' on the w.s. of the template.

PROBLEMS:

The cut edge of polystyrene sometimes appears jagged. This can be remedied by lightly sanding down.

The ink does not always adhere to the polystyrene. A WATER based ink should be used rather than an oil based ink/paint.

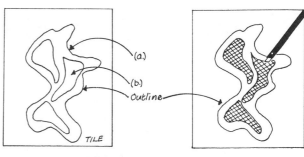

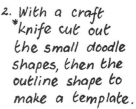

1. Using a pencil, draw a 'doodle' outline on a polystyrene tile (a.) Draw other 'doodles' inside the outline

2. With a craft *knife cut out the small doodle shapes, then the outline shape to make a template.

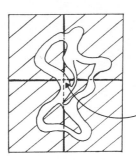

3. Mark the centre lines on the w.s. of the card. On the R.S. of the card mark the centre, by ruling lines vertically and horizontally.

Glue the template on to the R.S. of the card.

N.B. The design is reversed when printed

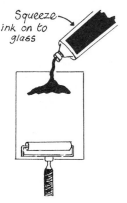

Squeeze ink on to glass

4. Use the glass to distribute the ink evenly over the roller.

5. Roll the ink EVENLY over the polystyrene template.

N.B. The roller should not touch the card.

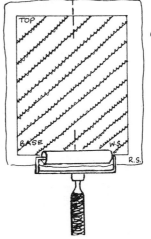

6. Mark the centre lines on the ironed fabric.
Turn over the template matching up the centre lines. Using a clean roller, roll evenly across the w.s. of the card.
* A milk bottle is a good substitute for a roller.

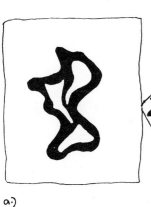

a.)

b.)

7. a.) Remove the template to produce a single print.
   b.) Continue printing to produce an all-over design.

Ideas: a.) SINGLE PRINT - motif on a bag or clothing. Enhanced with needleweaving and padded as a jewellery piece.
b.) ALL OVER DESIGN - fashion fabric, furnishing fabric (if colourfast ink is used).

10   Marbled patterns

Materials and Equipment	Craft or Fabric dyes (paint may also be used), plain cotton fabric without a dressing, glass, plastic, or acetate sheet, pipette (alternative—small plastic glue spatula), for embroidery—needle, scissors, embroidery threads, sewing machine.
Approximate Time	½ hour for marbling. 1 hour approximately for embroidery.
Age Group/Ability	From 11 years upwards. All abilities—according to the embroidery methods chosen.
Prerequisite Knowledge	• None for marbling. • For embroidery—knowledge of basic embroidery stitches or free-style embroidery using water-soluble fabrics.
Learning Activities	• The development of an aesthetic appreciation of colour, pattern, and the use of dye. • Working in the medium of dye or paint. • Skill and accuracy in the use of equipment and materials. • Using the imagination to achieve originality whilst working at a set task.
Assessment Criteria	• The ability to show skill and accuracy throughout the task. • The imaginative interpretation of the use of colour and dye in pattern. • To take the task one step further by adding an embroidery method which draws on previous knowledge, and the ability to demonstrate a skilful interpretation of that knowledge.
Development of the Project	• Introduction to the use of pattern in printing and further developments through other printing methods e.g. block, screen, etc. The use of colour and pattern in fashion and interior design.

HINTS:

1. The paint or dye must be the correct consistency. i.e. just thick enough to stop it spreading.
2. It is advisable to take 3 prints as each one gives a different effect and provides a greater choice as a background for embroidery.
3. When marbling ensure that the fabric is dropped directly on to the dye plate.

PROBLEMS:

The first print can be messy if too much dye is used. The second and third prints are usually the most interesting.

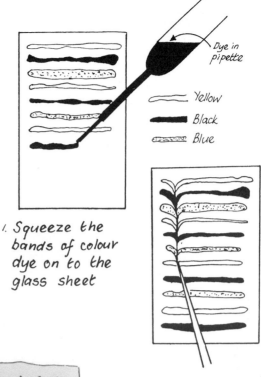

Dye in pipette

—— Yellow
—— Black
—— Blue

1. Squeeze the bands of colour dye on to the glass sheet

2. With the end of a paint brush, draw a line vertically to create a 'feather' pattern.

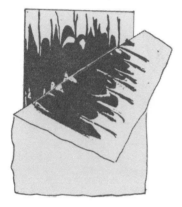

3. Drop the ironed fabric R.S. down on to the dye. Peel back a corner to check that a print has been made.

4. 1st print
The print can be heat sealed, by ironing between layers of paper.

2nd print, showing hand embroidery

3rd print, showing machine embroidery

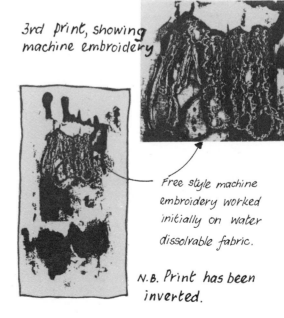

Hand embroidery using Cretan stitch and French Knots.

Free style machine embroidery worked initially on water dissolvable fabric.

N.B. Print has been inverted.

11 Spray-dyed padded frames

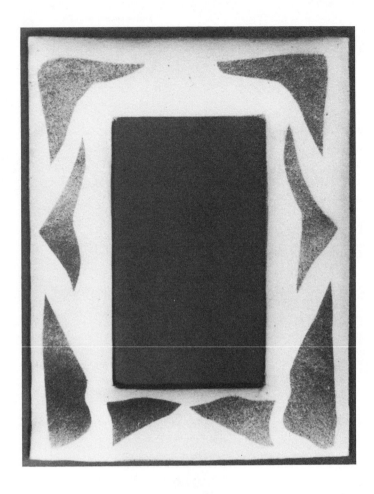

Materials and Equipment	Spray gun (or garden spray), calico—unbleached, wadding, Iron-on Vilene, paper to make stencil, cardboard for frame, paper to back frame, pencil, ruler, craft knife, needle, strong thread for lacing, fabric dye.
Approximate Time	2 hours.
Age Group/Ability	14 years upwards. Average ability.
Prerequisite Knowledge	The ability to recognise good design. An appreciation of colour.
Learning Activities	• Cutting a stencil. • The use and care of a spray gun. • The principles of making a padded article. • The interpretation of an original design, and the set work. • Introduction to mounting work by lacing. • Carrying out a task involving problem solving and decision making.
Assessment Criteria	• Accuracy and measurement in making a stencil and cutting a frame and fabric. • The correct use and care of the spray gun. • Skill in cutting out and applying the padding. • Lacing the frame using the correct method i.e. starting from the centre on each side, and mitring the corners last.
Development of the Project	Further investigation into the application of dye on to fabric and other materials by spray dyeing. The effective use of spray dyeing as a quick method in the making of costumes for the theatre, the home, in fashion, and as an embroidery background.

HINTS:

1. When designing the frame, begin at the corners first so that the design fits.
2. The spraygun should be directed on to a prepared upright surface rather than downwards if an even spray and sharp edged design is to be achieved.
3. The Blu-tack should not be visible on the R.S. of the stencil as it will distort the design line.
4. Thorough preparation of the surface to be used for spraydyeing is essential e.g. Newspaper cover.
5. The padded frame should not be laced too tightly, this causes crease lines on the R.S.

PROBLEMS:

Correct use of a spraygun requires practice. Alternatives = paint sprays for cars, garden sprays.

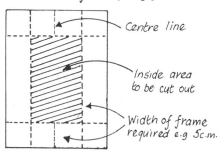

Centre line

Inside area to be cut out

Width of frame required e.g 5c.m.

1. Cut 1 A4 size paper = stencil
   Cut 1 A4 size card = frame

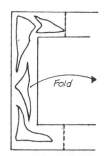

Fold

2. Draw the design at random on HALF the paper frame. Fold the frame in half, and trace through the remainder of the design.

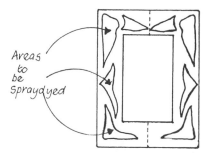

Areas to be spraydyed

3. Make a stencil by cutting out the areas to be spraydyed

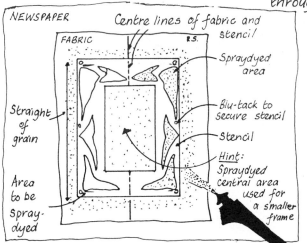

NEWSPAPER

FABRIC

R.S.

Centre lines of fabric and stencil

Spraydyed area

Blu-tack to secure stencil

Stencil

Hint: Spraydyed central area used for a smaller frame

Straight of grain

Area to be Spray-dyed

4. Press the background fabric and mark the centre lines lightly with tailors chalk. Line up the stencil with the fabric. Blu-tack the stencil down. Spray dye, directing the spray on to the stencil and moving the gun horizontally backwards and forwards.

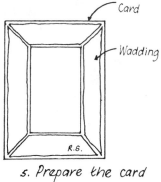

Card

Wadding

R.S.

5. Prepare the card frame by cutting out strips of wadding and glueing them to the R.S. of the frame.

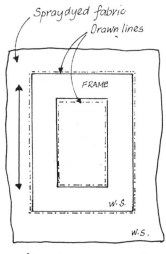

Spraydyed fabric

Drawn lines

FRAME

W.S.

W.S.

6. Place the prepared frame R.S. down on to the w.s. of the fabric, lining it up with the spraydyed fabric area. Draw round the inside and outside of the frame.

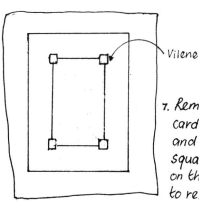

Vilene

7. Remove the card frame and press small squares of vilene on the fabric frame to reinforce the corners.

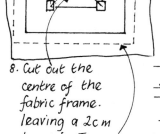

8. Cut out the centre of the fabric frame. leaving a 2cm turning. Trim down the outside edge to 2cm

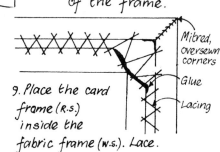

Mitred, Oversewn corners

Glue

Lacing

9. Place the card frame (R.S.) inside the fabric frame (w.s.). Lace.

N.B. The frame may be neatened on w.s. by a glued paper.

12   Splash bobbles

Materials and Equipment	Paint brush, craft/fabric dyes or paint, muslin, padding or Kapok, embroidery threads, needle, scissors, iron and board, card for mounting.
Approximate Time	1 hour (unmounted). Mounting takes ½ hour.
Age Group/Ability	13 years. Average ability.
Prerequisite Knowledge	Basic embroidery stitches e.g. running stitch, French knots.
Learning Activities	• An introduction to working with dyes, and their reaction to fabrics. • Using a simple dyeing method as a starting point for 3-D design and soft sculpture. • An introduction to the manipulation of fabric.

Assessment Criteria	• An imaginative use of colour and the application of dye.
	• Techniques and skills as follows:
	   1 the use of dye to present a blotched effect.
	   2 interpreting the dyed background into a 3-D form.
	   3 the use of embroidery in a skilful and effective way.
	• The interpretation and record of the task.

Development of the Project	Further investigation into dyes used as a background for embroidery methods; the reactions of different dyes on a variety of fabrics used for clothing and the home; other methods of dyeing fabrics, e.g. Batik, Tri-tik, tie and dye.

HINTS:
1. Bright colours give a more exciting result.
2. The paint or dye should be watered down if it will not spread on the muslin.
3. The splash dyeing can be dried by ironing between two layers of paper.
4. Strong cotton thread should be used for gathering.

PROBLEMS:

If the bobbles are overpadded it is difficult to embroider the French knots. Only a SELECTION of the folds falling from the gathers should be running stitched to give the soft 3D effect.

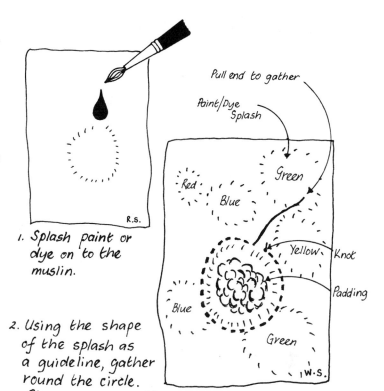

1. Splash paint or dye on to the muslin.

2. Using the shape of the splash as a guideline, gather round the circle. Place padding in the centre.

3. Pull up the circle as tightly as possible. Secure the thread end with a double back-stitch.

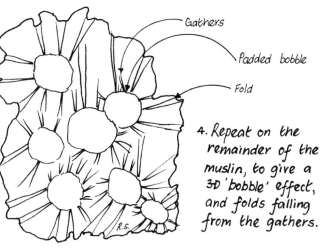

4. Repeat on the remainder of the muslin, to give a 3D 'bobble' effect, and folds falling from the gathers.

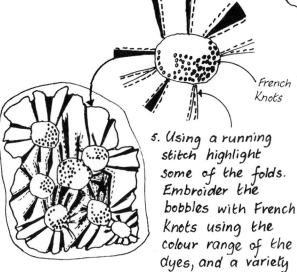

5. Using a running stitch highlight some of the folds. Embroider the bobbles with French knots using the colour range of the dyes, and a variety of threads.

6. Mount in a circular frame.

13 Tassel figures

Materials and Equipment	Oddments of wool and other yarns, 2 large beads, paper clip, waterproof pen, card.
Approximate Time	1 hour.
Age Group/Ability	13 years upwards, but the project could be simplified for a younger pupil.
Prerequisite Knowledge	An understanding of colour and texture, although this is not essential and it could be included in the project.
Learning Activities	<ul><li>The selection of appropriate yarns—decision making.</li><li>Dexterity in the use of yarns to produce a tassel.</li><li>The technique of making a tassel.</li></ul>
Assessment Criteria	<ul><li>The ability to carry out the set task to a high standard.</li><li>The ability to solve any problems that may arise.</li><li>The imaginative use of colour and texture.</li></ul>
Development of the Project	Tassels can be used on a variety of items made in textiles, e.g. as fringing, 3-D decoration on embroidery. The project also gives a basis for the pupil to explore the texture of threads and yarns, which could form the basis of an investigatory project.

1. The tassel threads can be wound around a book if card is unavailable.
2. A paper roll can be made and used to replace the bead :-

roll
hole left in centre

3. A variety of threads and yarns may be used.

PROBLEMS:
It is difficult to handle the tassel head when binding. Remedy= tape the head down on to card.

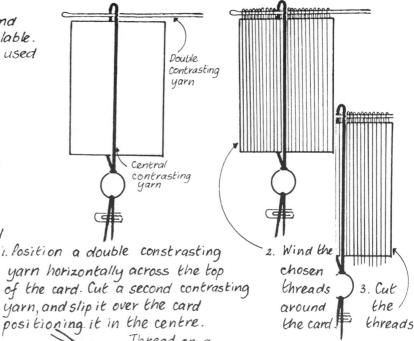

Double Contrasting yarn

Central contrasting yarn

1. Position a double constrasting yarn horizontally across the top of the card. Cut a second contrasting yarn, and slip it over the card positioning it in the centre.

2. Wind the chosen threads around the card.

3. Cut the threads

Thread on a bead. Secure with a paper clip.

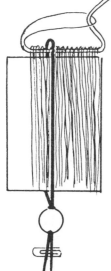

4. Make the horizontal contrasting yarn into a loop, drawing together the cut threads.

5. Slip all the threads off the card, pulling the loop tight.

6. Remove the paper clip, and slide the bead to the top of the yarn.
HINT: Tie a double knot to secure the position of the bead.

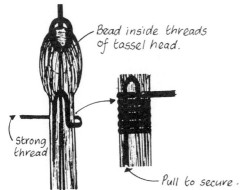

Bead inside threads of tassel head.

Strong thread

Pull to secure.

7. Place the two bands of threads together, covering the bead. Bind a strong thread around the base of the bead, to form a tassel.

9. Oversew the threads around the face.

8. Part the threads of the tassel head to reveal the 'face' area of the bead.

Layering

Beads

9. Using a waterproof pen add features to the face. Trim the tassel in layers. Add beads.

31

14   Tribal masks in macramé

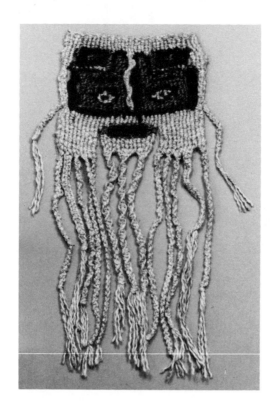

Materials and Equipment	Macramé string in 3 colours, or a selection of yarn/string, macramé board and pins (or the mask may be worked directly from a rod), plain drawing paper, graph paper, pencil, ruler, eraser. Optional: coloured pencils.
Approximate Time	Design 1 hour. Experimental/investigatory work 1 hour. Macramé 2 hours depending on the design.
Age Group/Ability	14 to 15 years. Above average ability.
Prerequisite Knowledge	• Basic macramé knots e.g. half knot, square or flat knot. • The ability to recognise and use design sources. • Previous experience in documenting, experimenting and investigating a task.
Learning Activities	• Encouraging inventiveness in original design. • Emphasising problem solving—by translating the design to give textural effects. • Introducing further macramé skills e.g. advanced knotting methods. • The use and manipulation of a variety of string or yarns.
Assessment Criteria	• The imaginative use of the design source. • The translation of a 2-D design into 3-D form. • Manipulative skills including the adaptation of previous knowledge. • The pupil's own evaluation of the project, the problems and the discoveries involved. • The investigation and research input by the pupil.
Development of the Project	Further research into macramé such as its origins, uses in fashion, in the home and as a craft. Investigation into other craft forms based on constructing a 'material' e.g. crochet, lace, etc. Making a large hanging using the tribal mask as the basis for an idea, that would include a range of threads, yarns, string and torn fabric. These could be dyed using vegetable dyes to give an authentic look.

HINTS:

1. This project has a thematic approach 'Designing from Headgear,' and could be interpreted into other textile forms.
2. The investigatory approach should be encouraged to include experimentation with basic knots, as well as the introduction of new macramé techniques.
3. Knots should be tried out with spare string before embarking on the main piece.
4. A macramé board is not essential, but does help to keep the string taut and aids knotting.

PROBLEMS:

The size of the design on graph paper is small in relation to the completed work. To calculate the size the experimental sample is compared with the graph –

1 knot = 1 square of the graph paper. The sizes of knots may vary according to the thickness of string being used.

1. Design Sources:-

Space Helmet   Biker's Helmet   Round heads Headwear

2. Research:-
The environment, media, magazines, museum.

3. Design taken from a Biker's helmet.

5. Experimentation with basic knots to translate the design e.g. using string and yarn of varying thickness and colour. Twisting fine and thick yarns together.

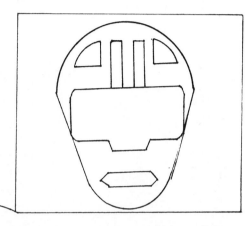

Tape
String and Yarn
Twisted Yarn (2 COLOURS)
Thick, woollen yarn.

4. Initial design is adapted and details are added.

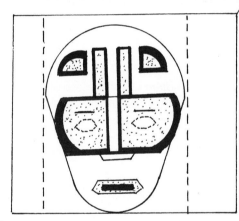

Vertical Clove Hitch ~ using cord

Flat or Square Knot ~ using mixed threads

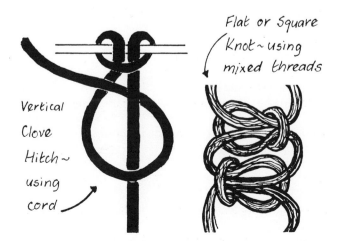

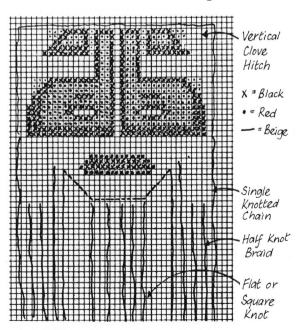

Vertical Clove Hitch

X = Black
• = Red
— = Beige

Single Knotted Chain

Half Knot Braid

Flat or Square Knot

33

15 Needleweaving stage

Materials and Equipment	Small card box, thin calico or lightweight cotton fabric, 1 piece of A4 card, PVA glue, scissors, fabric scraps, oddments of yarns and threads, threads for needleweaving, large-eyed needle.
Approximate Time	1 hour for the box and planning scenes. 2 hours for making scenes, adding needleweaving.
Age Group/Ability	13 years upwards, but the project could be simplified for younger age group.
Prerequisite Knowledge	• The ability to select and identify fabrics. • Some colour sense. • The ability to cut and measure accurately.
Learning Activities	• The selection of fabrics for textural effects. • The cutting, measuring, and covering of a box with fabric. • An introduction to needleweaving. • Working on a 3-D piece which also has perspective.
Assessment Criteria	• Skill in measuring, cutting, and covering the box. • The imaginative interpretation of a scene, together with the use of fabrics and threads. • The selection of appropriate fabrics and threads for the purpose. • The skilful and creative use of needleweaving. • The correct use of tools and equipment. • The appreciation of texture.
Development of the Project	Investigation and experimentation for textural effects with fabrics, yarns, and threads. Using needleweaving as an area for investigation e.g. as an ancient craft, and its revival for decorative use in the home.

HINTS:

1. The most useful boxes are those which contain notelets or lettercards, about 18c.m. x 10c.m.
2. The fabric to line the box looks most effective when painted in bands of colour with fabric dyes.
3. P.V.A. should be used for the glued areas, as it dries clear.
4. The 'landscape' card which fits inside the box, should be HALF the depth of the sides of the box.

PROBLEMS:

The 'warp' threads (No.7) should be taut, but not pulled tight — this distorts the box shape. Each 'warp' thread should be checked after it is attached.

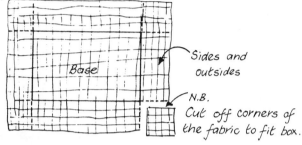

1. Using the box as a pattern, cut the fabric to fit the insides and the outsides e.g. BASE x SIDES x OUTSIDES

Base

Sides and outsides

N.B. Cut off corners of the fabric to fit box.

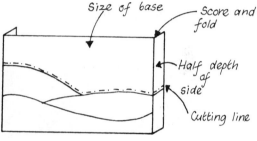

Size of base — Score and fold — Half depth of side — Cutting line

3. Cut a piece of card the size of the base of the box, plus half the depth, on both sides.
Draw lines on the card to represent a scene e.g. landscape. Cut away excess card.

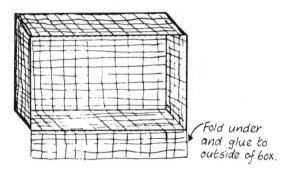

Fold under and glue to outside of box.

2. Glue the fabric inside the box, glueing the sides and outside.

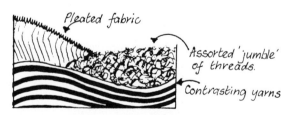

Pleated fabric

Assorted 'jumble' of threads.

Contrasting yarns

4. Translate the landscape into a textural form by experimenting with fabric, yarns, and threads. Select the materials to be used, and glue them on to the card.

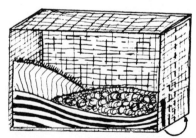

5. Glue the landscape inside the box by sliding it towards the BACK.

6. Using a strong thread, and uneven spacing sew across the front of the box, forming 'warp' threads

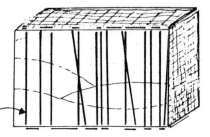

7. Needleweave across the 'warp' threads, to represent a woodland.
N.B. Beads may be included for extra effect.

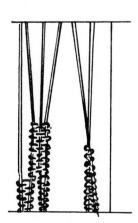

16 Acetate jewellery

Materials and Equipment

Transparent acetate (overhead projector sheet is the cheapest), sellotape, scissors, fine needle, fabric scraps and embroidery threads, beads, Vilene (iron on), jewellery fastenings.

Approximate Time

1 hour for the design and selection of materials.
1 hour to make a jewellery piece e.g. earrings.

Age Group/Ability

15 to 16 years. Average ability and above.

Prerequisite Knowledge

- A grounding in design.
- The ability to use colour imaginatively.
- A basic knowledge of embroidery.
- The skilful use of the sewing machine.

Learning Activities

- Designing a jewellery piece.
- Introducing a new medium in textiles e.g. acetate sheeting.
- The imaginative use of a variety of scrap materials.
- The imaginative use of embroidery for effect by machine or hand.
- To enable the pupil to link together fashion and accessories.

Assessment Criteria

- The ability to design and interpret the task, by decision making and problem solving, for example:
    1 making a template accurately.
    2 selecting threads and fabrics.
    3 using the acetate creatively and skilfully, including accuracy in cutting.
    4 selecting and experimenting with the embroidery method chosen, and documenting the task.

Development of the Project

Further investigation and experimentation into 'mixed media' jewellery, e.g. use of clay, washers, string.

HINTS:

1. Ideas and experimentations can be originally carried out by using paper.
2. Scissors should be used to cut the acetate rather than a craft knife which is not so easily controlled.
3. The acetate pieces can be sellotaped to paper after they are cut ~ to avoid mislaying them.

PROBLEMS:

Acetate should be carefully holepunched in the centre and edges, rather than pierced, as this causes splitting.

1. Choose a basic shape.

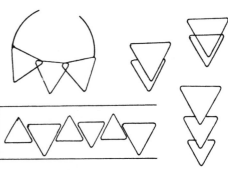

2. Experiment with the shape.

3. Make a template e.g. diamond shape chosen Mark the centre

4. Using scissors and template, cut out acetate shapes, making a small hole in centre.

5. Select fabrics, threads, and beads.

 6. Cut out the fabric, using the template.

 7. Sandwich between the acetate shapes.

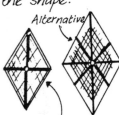 8. Using a fine thread, stitch through the centre hole.

Alternative

9. JEWELLERY SET - 4 pieces

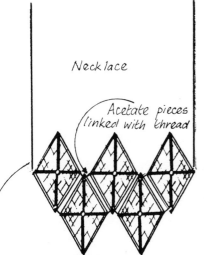

Necklace

Acetate pieces linked with thread

Wrapped thread over thin cord.

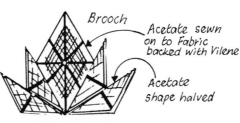

Brooch

Acetate sewn on to Fabric backed with Vilene

Acetate shape halved

Earrings

Fine thread

Beads

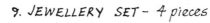

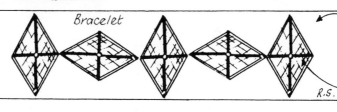

Bracelet

Fabric backed with Vilene

R.S.

Acetate sewn down

Further experimentation and ideas:-

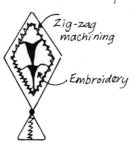

Zig-zag machining

Embroidery

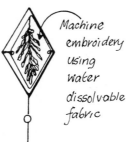

Machine embroidery using water dissolvable fabric

3 layer Acetate and fabric.

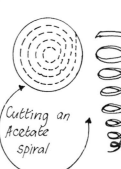

Cutting an Acetate spiral

17   One-stitch pictures

Materials and Equipment	Corduroy velvet, or any other fabric that has a regular line texture, wadding, a variety of threads and yarns (oddments), needle, tracing paper, embroidery hoop, paper for design, pencil.
Approximate Time	1 hour.
Age Group/Ability	12 years upwards, depending on the design chosen.
Prerequisite Knowledge	Prepared sketch or design.
Learning Activities	• The translation of a design into thread form. • Using the texture of a fabric as a basis for design interpretation. • Exploring and experimenting with the possibilities through the use and adaptation of one embroidery stitch. • To appreciate the influence that yarn and thread have on the appearance and texture of a stitch.
Assessment Criteria	• The choice of fabric as a background. • The originality and translation of the design. • The choice of embroidery stitch, and the method of experimentation to show imagination, and creativity. • Problem solving and decision making throughout the work. • The imaginative use of threads and colour.
Development of the Project	Further experimentation with embroidery stitches and backgrounds to achieve maximum effect.

HINTS:

1. Dark needlecord is difficult to work on as the cord lines cannot be clearly seen.
2. The needlecord should be used with the pile brushed downwards.
3. Block shapes are most suitable for the design.

PROBLEMS:

The needlecord must be kept taut in an embroidery ring, where long stitches are being used.

1. Original sketch is interpreted into a smooth outline form.

   Padded area

   Stitched areas

   N.B. The design may be transferred to the fabric by the 'prick and pounce chalk method. The use of hairspray prevents the chalk lines smudging.

2. Translation into padded areas, and those to be stitched.

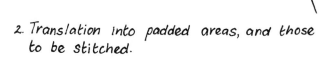

3. Experimentation with ONE* stitch, and a selection of threads:-

▭	Padded area	▮	Twisted Yarn
- - -	Stab stitching	‖	Soft wool
|	Thick thread		
¦	Single fine thread	‖	2 colour thread
⦙	Knotted thread		
⌇	Textured Yarn	⫼	3 colour thread
			Threads are split and mixed.

*e.g. stitch selected = STRAIGHT STITCH

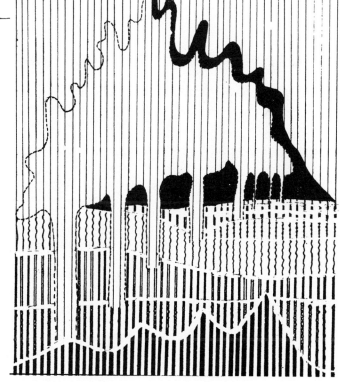

18 Canvas greetings

Materials and Equipment	Card (double the size of the finished greetings card), canvas, embroidery threads, needle, waterproof felt pen, PVA glue, pencil, coloured pencils/paints (optional), source material (for ideas) such as children's books, comics, catalogues, embroidery books.
Approximate Time	Design: 1 hour. Canvas work: 1 hour. Card: 1 hour.
Age Group/Ability	15 to 16 years. Average ability.
Prerequisite Knowledge	• Some knowledge of children and child care would be an advantage. • Appreciation of design and colour. • Basic knowledge of embroidery methods.
Learning Activities	• Researching and selecting a subject for design work. • Translating the design into one suitable for a card, and to show an embroidery technique not previously taught. • Carrying out the embroidery technique in a methodical way.
Assessment Criteria	• The ability to research, and select knowledge. • Translating the knowledge into a practical form i.e. design, greetings card. • Choosing an appropriate textile technique. • The skilful use of tools and fabric, and the careful execution of the task.
Development of the Project	Development into the investigation of any other embroidery methods, or further investigation into canvas work including traditional and modern techniques. The project can also be developed by its obvious connections with child care, e.g. using the design again for another item.

HINTS:

1. Masking or adhesive tape may be placed around the edge of the canvas to stop it fraying.
2. Both designs must line up ACCURATELY.
3. The cut out piece of card from the window must be trimmed back 2 m.m. all round before using it to mount the canvas work.
4. Both the design and the canvas work should be kept as simple as possible.
5. To speed up the making process, the card may be left in monochrome.

PROBLEMS:

Accuracy is essential in a) cutting the window b) mounting the canvas work c) attaching the canvas work to the card so that it can be clearly seen through the window.

Design A

'Humpty Dumpty', sat on a wall.....

Design B

1. Using the source material, draw two designs that show a sequence.
A = for card front   B = for inside card
Transfer the design on to a folded piece of card:-

HINT: Score the card on the outside before folding

Design A

Design B (inside card)

OPTIONAL: Colour the card using paints.

2. Mark out a window area on the front of the card.

3. Cut out the window area using a craft knife. Draw the window position LIGHTLY on to the inside of the card.

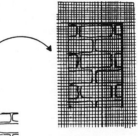

4. Place the cut out window behind the canvas R.S. uppermost. Using a waterproof felt pen draw through the design.

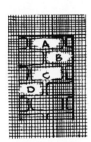

5. Translate the area into canvas work stitches:-
   A. Tent stitch   B. Brick stitch   c. Cross stitch   D. Diagonal Satin stitch.

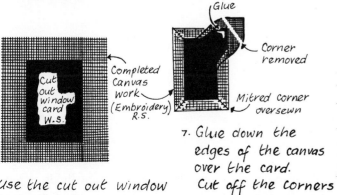

Cut out window card W.S.

Completed Canvas work (Embroidery) R.S.

Glue

Corner removed

Mitred corner oversewn

6. use the cut out window to mount the canvas work, placing the R.S. of the card to the w.s. of the embroidery.

7. Glue down the edges of the canvas over the card. Cut off the corners and mitre.
N.B. The canvas work should be stretched and pressed before mounting.

8. Glue the canvas work into position inside the card.

19   Suffolk puff box

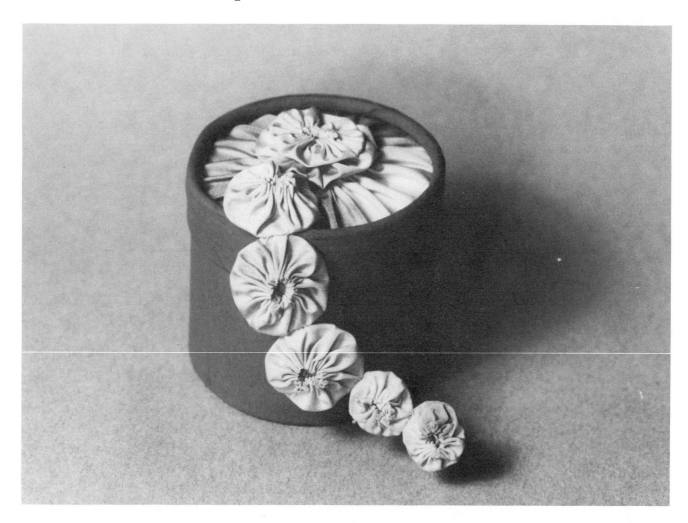

Materials and Equipment	Box (see working method), fabric scraps e.g. lightweight fabrics, paper for pattern templates, needle, threads, scissors.
Approximate Time	1 hour.
Age Group/Ability	11 years upwards. All abilities.
Prerequisite Knowledge	None.
Learning Activities	An introduction to: • The covering of a 3-D form. • Patchwork e.g. Suffolk Puffs. • Making a pattern template, including measuring and accuracy. • Choosing fabrics and threads. • The evaluation of the completed work including problems arising etc.
Assessment Criteria	• The originality in interpretation of the task. • Problem solving in pattern making. • Decision making in the choice of colour, fabric and thread. • The skill and aptitude shown in making the Suffolk Puffs and their decorative use on the box.
Development of the Project	Further investigation into other traditional forms of patchwork, e.g. log cabin, shell. The relationship between the origins of patchwork and the home.

HINTS:

1. Any round box having a removable lid and base made of card can be used e.g. dusting powder box, chocolate box, pill box, some spice containers. Any size may be used.
2. The fabrics used should be lightweight e.g. cotton lawn, acetate lining, silk.

PROBLEMS:

The small Suffolk Puffs may prove difficult to handle, and can be easily mislaid.
To remedy both these problems one Puff should be attached to another as soon as it is made.

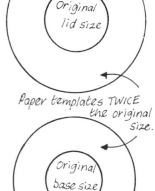

1. Using the lid and base as a pattern cut:—

Paper templates TWICE the original size.

2. Using the templates cut in fabric:—
3 lids, 3 bases, 1 enlarged lid, 1 enlarged base. (8 pieces)

a.) 3 templates of lid   b.) 3 templates of base

c.) 1 template each from the top and base TWICE their original size

3. Using the fabric for the lid, gather round the turned in edge. Place the lid in the centre of the fabric. Draw up, securing with a back-stitch. Repeat using the fabric base.

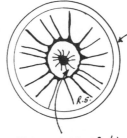

OPTIONAL:—
The lid may be padded, before the Suffolk Puff is secured.

4. Using one of the fabric circles cut the original size of the lid, make a small Suffolk Puff to slip-stitch in the centre of the completed lid.

5. Place the covered lid back into the lip of the lid, and the covered base into the box.

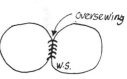

6. Make up the remaining 5 fabric circles. Join the Puffs together by oversewing, and attach to the lid of the box

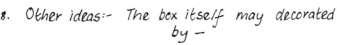

8. Other ideas:— The box itself may decorated by —

7. Completed box using small Puffs in various sizes for decoration.

Bands of ribbon.

Lace

Patterned Fabric

Paint

20 **Party mask card**

Materials and Equipment	Tracing paper, white card (or white paper glued on to cereal box card), coloured pencils/crayons or paint, pencil, eraser, ruler, Iron-on Vilene, felt, fabric scraps, assorted embroidery threads, machine cottons, needle, pins, scissors, iron, ironing board.
Approximate Time	Design 1 hour. Mask approximately 2 hours.
Age Group/Ability	15 to 16 years. Average ability.
Prerequisite Knowledge	• The colour wheel. • The basic principles of design. • A basic knowledge of embroidery stitches. • Some experience of the pre-school child (this is an idea that links well with child care).
Learning Activities	• The use of knowledge of colour, shape, and texture. • Problem solving—in the choice and appreciation of appropriate fabrics and embroidery techniques. • Skills—cutting out, construction techniques. • Research into the suitability of the card and mask for a pre-school child.
Assessment Criteria	• The design and its imaginative translation. • Manipulative skills including embroidery, attachment of elastic, use of tools. • Decision making—the selection of suitable materials and techniques. • Recording, testing, and observing (evidence that the task has been thought through).
Development of the Project	The mask could motivate further investigation into designing and making clothing items for children which can be linked to child care and development, plus research into child-related consumerism. Masks as a theatrical costume. Investigation into theatre costume, e.g. principal characters who wear masks.

HINTS:

1. Bright colours are most suitable when designing for children.
2. Velcro provides an easy fastening for the mask.
3. Felt pens and coloured pencils do not give such a good result as painting the card. Pens and pencils do not provide easy and even coverage.
4. The card itself may be in monochrome, whilst the mask is brightly coloured.
5. 'Colourphelt' or painted Vilene (Firm-Iron-on) fused together may be used as a cheap substitute for felt.

PROBLEMS:

The slit in the card (to house the mask) may tear. This can be strengthened by placing adhesive tape on the w.s. of the card before cutting the slit.

3. Character details are added to the basic design.

MAKING the MASK:

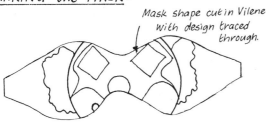

Mask shape cut in Vilene with design traced through.

a) Cut the mask shape out in Vilene (iron-on) Iron the Vilene mask on to the background of FELT. Cut out.
  Cut a second mask shape in Vilene, with W.S. upwards. Using a fabric pen, trace the design lines through the Vilene.

R.S. of Vilene section (eye)   W.S. of Fabric scrap

b) Cut the Vilene into sections of the design. Iron the sections on to the selected fabric scraps.

1. Basic design for Mask person, using circles and ruled lines.

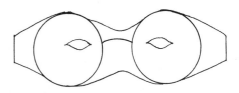

2. Basic shape for mask, taken from spectacles. Cut ONE in tracing paper to make a template.

Fold of card (outwards)

Slit to house mask

Template showing mask design

4. The card design is completed and coloured. Check the tracing paper mask template against the card. Trace through the design details of the mask.

c) Appliqué the fabrics to the background. Enhance with embroidery stitches. Oversew elastic to one side of the mask, using Velcro or a hook on the remaining side to attach the elastic.

21   **Smocked abstracts**

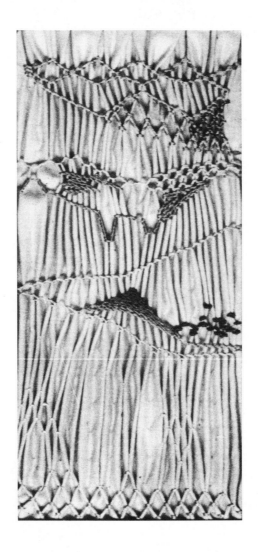

Materials and Equipment	Background fabric (any plain fabric that will retain ironed-in crease lines e.g. cotton), fabric marker, needle, iron and board, embroidery threads, embroidery books—used as reference for smocking stitches.
Approximate Time	1 to 2 hours depending on the amount of smocking required.
Age Group/Ability	13 years upwards. Average ability.
Prerequisite Knowledge	Basic principles of the use of sewing tools and equipment.
Learning Activities	<ul><li>Drawing a random design.</li><li>The basic principles involved in smocking, using traditional stitches, but not a traditional method.</li><li>The manipulation of fabric to provide a surface for smocking.</li><li>The introduction and exploration of smocking stitches.</li></ul>
Assessment Criteria	<ul><li>The use of sewing tools and equipment.</li><li>The manipulation of fabric accurately e.g. folding.</li><li>Imaginative random design and its suitability for the purpose.</li><li>The selection of smocking stitches to interpret the design, and problem solving through experimentation with stitches.</li></ul>
Development of the Project	The further use of smocking on other clothing and home furnishings. Investigation into smocking, for example, the traditional method, its history.

HINTS:

1. The width of pleats chosen can be of any size, but the work looks most effective when narrow folds are used.
2. The pleat or fold width must be uniform throughout.
3. If a colour wash is used on the fabric, this will produce markings which can be used as the basis of the random design.
4. The traditional method of smocking may be introduced after pressing the folded fabric, by picking up the folds and tacking across.

PROBLEMS:

The amount of fabric used should be three times the required finished size. The fabric folds must be held in place whilst working – a large safety pin at the top and bottom of the work can be used to secure the folds.

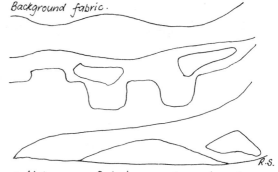

Background fabric.

R.S.

1. Using a fabric marker draw lines and shapes at random on to the background fabric.
OPTIONAL:- The fabric may be colour washed.

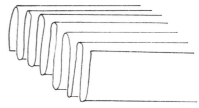

2. Fold the fabric into narrow pleats.

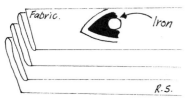

Fabric.   Iron

R.S.

3. Press the pleated folds with a hot iron.

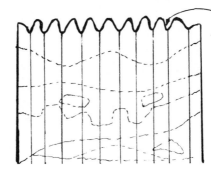

4. Open up the fabric, then hold the folds pressing them together again.
Examine the lines on the fabric, note that they are now distorted.

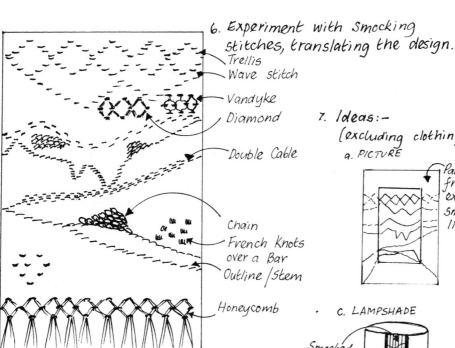

6. Experiment with Smocking stitches, translating the design.

Trellis
Wave stitch
Vandyke
Diamond
Double Cable
Chain
French Knots over a Bar
Outline/Stem
Honeycomb

7. Ideas:-
(excluding clothing)
a. PICTURE

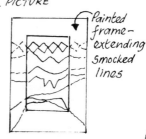

Painted frame- extending smocked lines

b. 3D PIECE

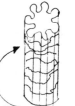

Free standing textural interpretation e.g. tree trunk design.

c. LAMPSHADE

Smocked panel

22   Line and stitch fashion

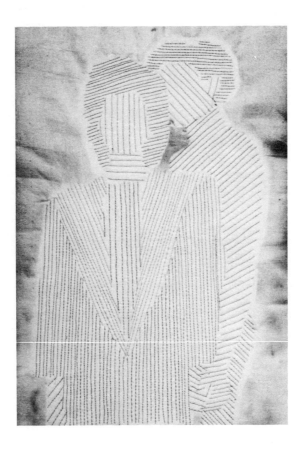

Materials and Equipment	Design sources (such as fashion books, magazines, papers, pattern books, advertising and the media), paper, pencil, ruler, eraser, coloured pencils/pens, Calico, muslin, polyester wadding (optional), machine cottons, sewing machine (hand or electric). Optional: fabric dyes, diffuser or spray gun.
Approximate Time	Design 1 hour. Machine work (*excluding* spray dyeing) approximately 1½ hours.
Age Group/Ability	13 years. Average ability, but the idea can also be simplified for 11 year olds.
Prerequisite Knowledge	• Threading the machine correctly. • The ability to recognise the correct tension.
Learning Activities	• Designing from a traced shape. Use of colour and line. • Sewing-machine skills, including stitch length and thread experimentation. • The use of design, including its application and interpretation into thread form. • The use of sewing tools.
Assessment Criteria	• The interpretation of the design, and the use of colour. • The use of the sewing machine in a competent manner. • Choosing the appropriate thread and stitch lengths for the task. • Accuracy in machine stitching. • The translation of the set task, including its execution.
Development of the Project	It forms a basis for machine skills which can be developed in all areas of textiles. The design used could be a decoration on clothing, e.g. on a pocket, or as an embroidery in itself. It provides an introduction to further investigative work to increase an understanding of the scope of the sewing machine e.g. machine attachments and built-in functions.

HINTS:

1. Muslin provides a cheap alternative to calico as the background fabric.
2. Threads of different thicknesses (30, 40, 50) encourage experimentation in needle, tension, and stitch size. (One stitch size only may be used to speed up the project.)
3. The shapes in the design must be large enough to be translated into machine lines.

PROBLEMS:

The securing of machine ends is time consuming. A few can be secured, whilst the remaining can be taped with adhesive on the w.s. of the work.

1. Trace outlines of original drawing.

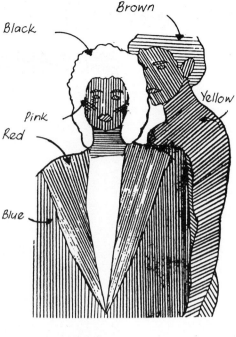

2. Select line directions and colours. Rule in using straight lines.

Cotton background

3. Transfer design on to a cotton background using a felt pen.

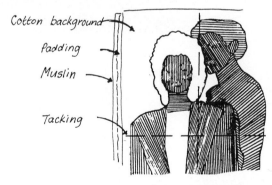

Cotton background
Padding
Muslin
Tacking

4. Tack the prepared background to a layer of padding and muslin. Machine lines in colours and directions of the design using varying lengths of machine stitches.

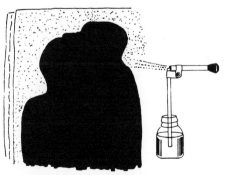

5. (OPTIONAL) Mask out machined area, and diffuse using a fabric dye.

23 Diffused and quilted patterns

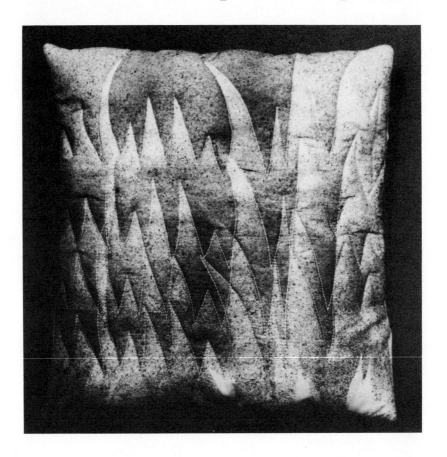

Materials and Equipment	Newspaper, fabric dyes or paint, Blu-tack, machine cotton, background fabric (calico), padding (preferably iron-on), diffuser, iron and board, sewing machine, scissors.
Approximate Time	1 hour for diffusing. 1 hour for quilting, depending on the design.
Age Group/Ability	11 years upwards. Suitable for the complete ability range, as the quilting can be simplified.
Prerequisite Knowledge	None.
Learning Activities	• Using the sewing machine, i.e. threading, choice of stitch, stitching accurately, using the machine to enhance a design. • The preparation and use of a diffuser. • Designing a random pattern choice and use of colour and dyes. • An introduction to quilting.
Assessment Criteria	• Skill and accuracy in the use of the diffuser and the sewing machine. • The working method in diffusing and stitching. • The interpretation of the task, and documenting an account of the procedure and results.
Development of the Project	Using the sewing machine for other decorative techniques, leading to the use of machine attachments. Experimentation into other methods of using dye on fabric as a background for machining. The finished diffused and quilted work may be developed further by making it into a small herbal cushion as shown in the illustration.

HINTS:

1. It is easier to control the spray of the diffuser if it is blown directly ahead e.g. stencil or template is placed on a wall.
2. The diffusing may be dried quickly with the use of a hairdryer.
3. Practice diffusing before spraying the work.
4. The colour changes are not always definite between the patterns. The machine lines are then stitched at random.

PROBLEMS:

The newspaper template becomes soggy after frequent use, but is a cheap substitute for card.

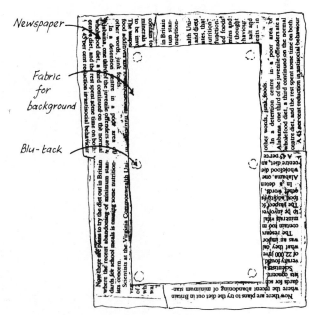

1. Prepare the wall/table by covering with newspaper. Blu-tack the ironed fabric to the newspaper.

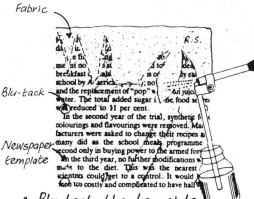

2. Tear or cut the edge of the newspaper at random, making a template.

3. Blu-tack the template to the background fabric. Diffuse with the first colour.

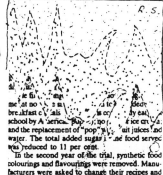

4. Move the template and re-position. Spray on second colour with diffuser.
   - - - - - - denotes colour change.

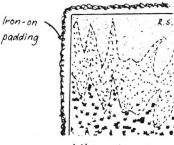

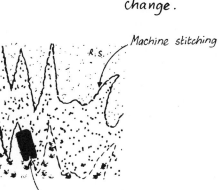

5. Move template again, re-position. Spray with 3rd colour. Continue using 4 colours.

6. When dry, iron padding on to w.s. of fabric.

Idea: Method used on a Herbal cushion

24   Land and sea scapes

Materials and Equipment	Fabric scraps,* machine cottons, cotton fabric or muslin, card or thick paper, glue, sewing machine, scissors, needles, pins, fabric pen or tailor's chalk. *Access should be given to a 'scrap box'.
Approximate Time	2 hours. 1 hour for the preparation and selection of fabrics. 1 hour for machining and mounting.
Age Group/Ability	13 to 14 years, but the project could be simplified for a younger age range.
Prerequisite Knowledge	• Basic knowledge of the machine i.e. threading up, bobbin winding, stitch alteration. • Basic knowledge of fabrics.
Learning Activities	• The identification of fabrics. • The manipulation of fabrics, and appreciation of colour and texture. • The use of the sewing machine i.e. automatic embroidery stitches or zig-zag. • The choice and use of equipment appropriate for the purpose, e.g. needle and threads.
Assessment Criteria	• The aesthetic appreciation of shape, colour and texture. • Skill in the management of limited resources. • Adjusting the machine for embroidery work. • Experimentation with and choice of machine work. • Effectiveness in fulfilling the planned work, and recording it systematically.
Development of the Project	Introduction to machine embroidery leading into freestyle work. Using fabrics suitable for a variety of purposes, investigatory work. Designing from land and sea scapes to produce a 3-D embroidery form.

HINTS:
1. Fabrics look most effective when chosen in shades and tones of one colour, but a variety of textures.
2. The background alternative ~ paper may be used.

PROBLEMS:
The automatic embroidery stitches chosen must compliment the line of the design.

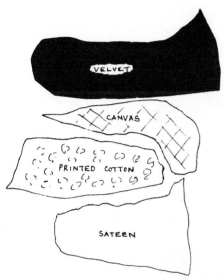

1. Select fabric scraps, identifying the material. Place fabrics together experimenting with colour and texture.

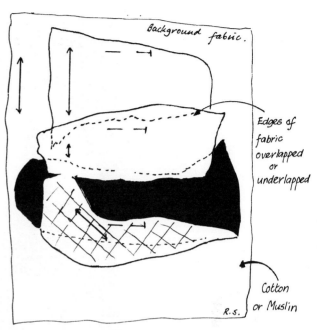

2. Arrange fabric scraps to form an interesting land or sea scene. Mark straight of grain on W.S. of fabrics. Use some fabrics on the straight of grain and some on the bias for extra effect. Pin.

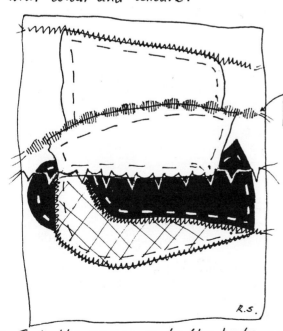

3. Tack the scraps on to the background fabric. Machine across the work where the scraps join or overlap, using a range of automatic embroidery stitches.

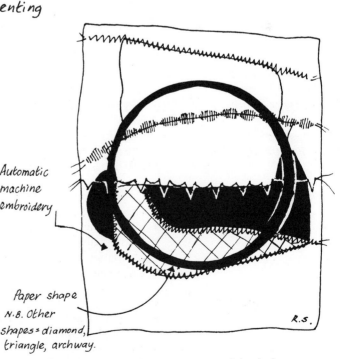

4. Using a paper shape, identify an interesting area of the embroidery. Cut a mount in paper. Sandwich the embroidery by glueing it between the paper mount and a cardboard backing.

25   **Pocket hanging**

Materials and Equipment	Plain fabric, e.g. Cotton, cotton polyester, backing fabric, needle, pins, tacking cotton, fabric marker, embroidery threads, sewing machine, iron and board.
Approximate Time	Design 1 hour. Application of pockets 2 hours.
Age Group/Ability	13 years upwards. Above average ability. NB A 'one pocket' hanging may be made with lower abilities.
Prerequisite Knowledge	• The use of the sewing machine. • Use of basic equipment and sewing tools.
Learning Activities	• Designing by using a clothing construction process as a basis. • The making and application of two types of pocket. • Interpreting an original design. • Manipulative skills such as cutting out a pattern, and loops. • Machining—selection of the correct stitch and tension. • Embroidery.
Assessment Criteria	• A pleasing design, with thought for its interpretation. • The choice and construction of pockets. • The application and machining of pockets. • The cutting of fabric to make loops. • The selection and execution of embroidery.
Development of the Project	Making clothing using pockets as a style feature. Investigation into types of pockets, e.g. through history, in theatrical costuming. Developing other machine skills in the construction of clothing and articles for the home.

HINTS:

1. The pocket types should be chosen first and should be of a workable size.
2. The hanging should be based on basic face shapes e.g. oval, round, etc.
3. It is important to press the pockets after each stage of construction.

PROBLEMS:

It may be difficult to embroider the hanging after the pockets have been applied. Basic embroidery can be added to the pockets before they are made up.

PATCH POCKETS

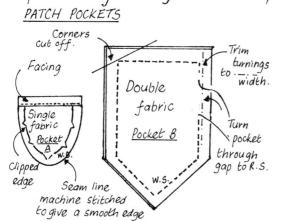

3. Make up the two pocket types:-
Pocket A (for 'Eyes') cut 2, Pocket B (for 'Nose' or 'Beak') Cut 2 for double fabric pocket.

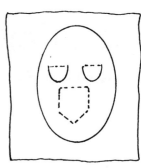

1. Draw the face shape on to the background fabric using a fabric pen.

2. Mark the positions of the pockets.

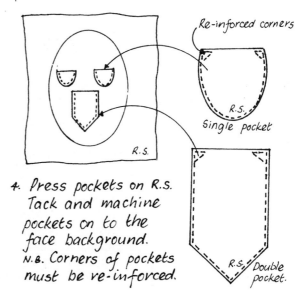

4. Press pockets on R.S. Tack and machine pockets on to the face background.
N.B. Corners of pockets must be re-inforced.

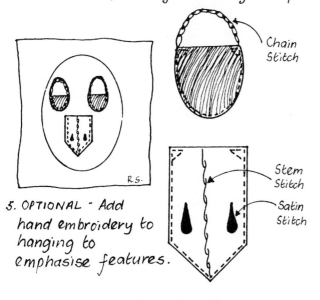

5. OPTIONAL - Add hand embroidery to hanging to emphasise features.

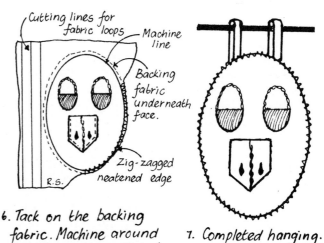

6. Tack on the backing fabric. Machine around the face shape. Trim to machine line; zig-zag the edge. With the spare fabric, make and attach the loops for hanging.

7. Completed hanging.

Ideas:

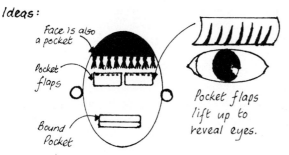

Pocket flaps lift up to reveal eyes.

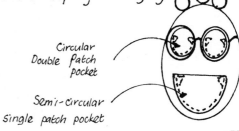

Circular Double Patch pocket

Semi-circular single patch pocket

Planning and Executing a Complete Project—A Working Example

This final chapter shows how some of the ideas and projects in the earlier chapters can be brought together as a set brief to include the common element and the child care areas of Home Economics.

Any such major project should be seen by the teacher to fall into three distinct stages:

1 thinking and planning,
2 making and process,
3 evaluation: a) by the pupil, and b) by the teacher.

As these major projects are designed to be used as part of a GCSE Textiles programme, the teacher should ensure that these stages are translated into an assessment grid which satisfies the requirements of the relevant examination board.

The Brief: An Example

'Design and make a suitable hanging for a young child's room. The hanging should show a range of textile techniques.'

First Stage: Thinking and Planning

When examining the brief the following should be established before the investigatory process can take place:

a) the age and sex of the young child,
b) the existing decor of the room.

In determining the age and sex of the child the pupil may choose someone that he or she knows. The pupil can then proceed to investigate the child's likes and dislikes to determine what would appeal. On the other hand, a pupil using an imaginary child could base his or her research more in consumerism, e.g. children's shops, the media, all of which provide good source material for establishing what currently sells or appeals to the chosen age group and sex (bright colours, bold shapes, recognisable characters from fiction and so on).

The existing decor means not only the colours and furniture already in the room, but also such things as aspect and room shape and size. Once again it would be possible to design the hanging for a known room or for an imagined one. In the latter case some initial research into decorating rooms suitable for young children would prove useful.

Documentation of the above, to include notes on children observed at play or in conversation, may be compiled in a folder and later referred to as source material during the design process.

The brief is now ready to be studied again with the teacher encouraging the pupil to consider how the requirements of the brief can be best fulfilled. But which comes first, the design or the textile techniques? In most cases solutions will be design led, and two immediate decisions will therefore have to be taken:

a) is the hanging to be 'ageless' in that it can continue to be part of the decor of the room long after the child has grown up? and

b) is the hanging to be purely decorative, or functional, or educational, or a mixture of all three?

Once the subject matter for the hanging design has been chosen, (e.g. a character from a nursery rhyme) further research, planning and decision making takes place. This could be in the form of looking at a range of children's books and magazines to compare the different drawings and design conceptions of nursery rhyme (and other) child-centred characters. In this way a clearer idea of how to design a version of a nursery rhyme character may start to form in the pupil's mind.

Let us suppose that the pupil has chosen the nursery rhyme 'Boys and Girls come out to Play', and wishes to use a character from this rhyme as the basis for the textile hanging. The emphasis on play (in the title) gives the pupil a design lead—the character to be depicted should be playing, swinging on a bar for example. Thus, a basic shape for the overall design begins to emerge (see the drawing opposite).

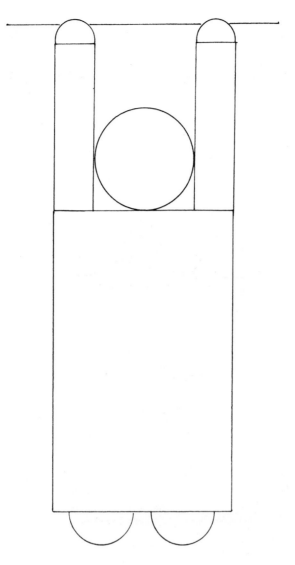

Basic design drawn from circles and oblongs

Once the basic design has been drawn out, translation into textile techniques can then begin as, for example, in the design for Swinging Sidney (see the drawing overleaf).

Although the initial design has now been decided, this does not necessarily mean that it is fixed. It may well be found, through experimentation, that the proposed fabrics and techniques are not wholly suitable and, therefore, the plan is in need of some modification or rethinking. I would suggest that the following five points, at least, need careful consideration when selecting fabrics:

    a) safety (burning test),
    b) laundering qualities (colourfastness, crease resistance, shrinkage, etc.),
    c) handling and draping qualities,
    d) strength and durability (ability to withstand wear and a child's play),
    e) cost (working within a prescribed budget).

These factors should be researched, considered and documented. The results of this activity would then enable the pupil to make a more informed choice and selection of fabrics with which to work the design.

At the same time as confirming a fabric's suitability judged against the above five criteria, the pupil must give equal consideration to the demands of the techniques and processes to be involved in creating the hanging itself. This may involve further experimentation and the making of samples, but inherent in the idea of working on a major project or brief is the notion of using previously documented knowledge. Any problem-solving or decision-making conclusions should be recorded with these samples.

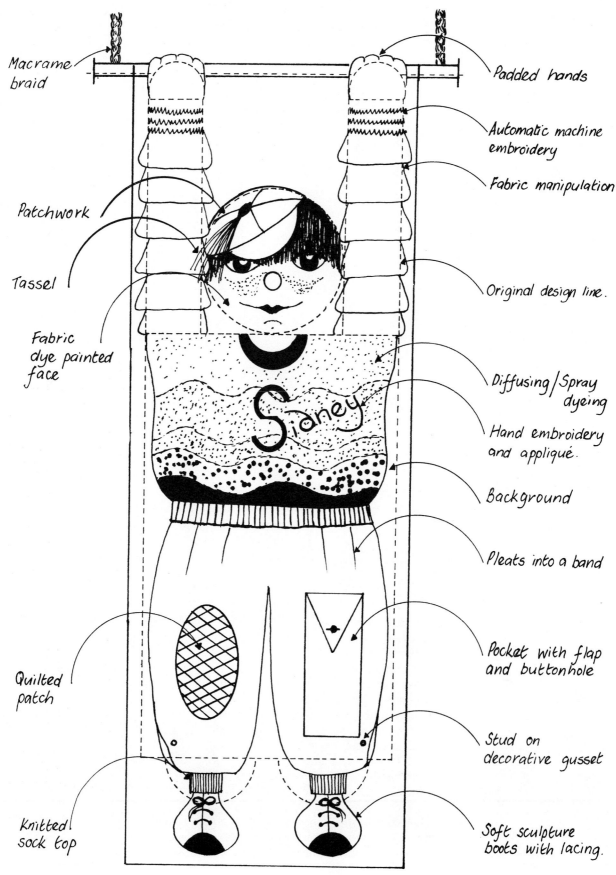

Macrame braid

Padded hands

Automatic machine embroidery

Fabric manipulation

Patchwork

Tassel

Original design line.

Fabric dye painted face

Diffusing / Spray dyeing

Hand embroidery and appliqué.

Background

Pleats into a band

Quilted patch

Pocket with flap and buttonhole

Stud on decorative gusset

Knitted sock top

Soft sculpture boots with lacing.

Sidney

N.B. Only a SELECTION of these techniques would be used in the project.

The samples in themselves are not the whole experimentation process, since the pupil also needs to decide upon the most suitable tools, equipment and materials for each purpose, for example the correct thread, tension and machine stitch. A rough plan or sequence could be drawn up by the pupil to show the proposed order of work. Timing is all important here. The brief will most probably involve a time limit and so the pupil must select techniques that also take this factor into account.

Second Stage: Making and Process

A working plan for the construction of 'Swinging Sidney'

Stage 1 Prepare the background fabric.

Stage 2 Transfer the design.

Stage 3 Divide the design into individual working areas, according to the techniques being used.

Stage 4 Work through each technique area, thereby making up the individual parts, e.g. soft sculpture for the head, hands and feet.

Stage 5 Construct Sidney by sewing each individual part to the background in a systematic way, beginning with the head.

Stage 6 Completion.

During each of these stages the teacher should continually assess whether the pupil is:

a) working methodically,

b) showing an ability to translate the design from drawing into the medium of textiles,

c) solving problems as they arise,

d) demonstrating a range of techniques and processes,

e) capable of executing the techniques and processes to a prescribed standard.

Although the pupil has initiated an investigatory programme in order to interpret the given brief successfully, adjustments may still need to be made either to alter the design or to modify the chosen techniques. Similarly, the pupil may wish to add further ideas to the work or to supplement one idea with another. The brief in this example calls for an imaginative interpretation, together with the demonstration of a range of skills. Although the brief has been labelled a *design* brief, the investigatory process is still the important factor. The emphasis here shows that particular regard should be paid to the *processes* involved in arriving at the end product, rather than merely judging or assessing the merits of the end product itself. This is not to deny the value of producing a finished item to a high standard, but rather to see it in a clear relation to the working processes involved. In other words, the standard of work expected during the making process should be established by the teacher in such a way that promotes activity rather than inhibits it. This may be achieved in the following ways:

i) try to establish working standards from the very start (i.e. using previous work),

ii) make the textiles room as interesting and stimulating as possible by having resources, samples and other general items continually available and visible,

iii) encourage continuous self-evaluation by each pupil and through group discussion,

iv) as a teacher, try to adopt more of the role of enquirer rather than dictator and expert: encourage the pupil to resolve a problem rather than expect to be given the solution.

The teacher must achieve a balance. Although each and every method or technique promoted by the teacher throughout the course will depend to some extent on defined procedure, it is important not to inhibit the pupil's creative development by over-emphasising particular techniques.

The final response to the brief should be presented as follows:

1 the finished item displayed;

2 the experimental and investigatory work, notes, sources of information, order of work etc., presented together in a logical format, for example in a folder;

3 a self-assessment and evaluation sheet made available.

Third Stage: Evaluation

Evaluation of the pupil's response to the brief.

The work detailed above was divided into a sequence of identifiable stages. Each of these stages should be recorded separately by the teacher. One way of doing this is by a flow chart that allows space for assessment at each stage. The investigatory and problem-solving processes are also accounted for in this method of assessment.

An assessment checklist for both pupil and teacher should include the following:

a) a list of the skills needed and used to respond to the brief (e.g. verbal communication of ideas, use of logic in tackling problems and identifying reasons, sharing resources).

b) an account of how the skills were used.

c) a record of any experiments or investigations.

d) an assessment of whether the brief has actually been met by the work produced.

Questions that pupils may ask themselves would include:

a) which stages was I good at?

b) which stages did I find required further experience?

c) if I could do this project again, what changes, improvements or modifications would I make?

d) did I translate the brief satisfactorily?

e) are there any ideas or techniques that I would now like to develop further?

Self-assessment sheets may be devised which list the various stages of the work and which require pupil response in the form of a ticked or crossed box against each question. The pupils should also be expected to write a brief evaluation, in their own words, of the whole project.

The teacher's evaluation includes a study of the continual assessment programme together with marking the finished item. The marks for the finished item will be minimal compared to those awarded for the planning and making stages, where the set skills are important. The teacher may assess the attainment of the pupil in working through this project as follows:

a) an ability to instigate a programme of relevant research;

b) an ability to record and select the products of such research;

c) an ability to respond to different stimuli (e.g. ideas arising from personal research, experimentation, or from working with or talking to others);

d) an ability to adapt, refine and modify ideas and techniques;

e) an ability in chosen skills, methods or techniques;

f) an ability to work having consideration for personal safety and the safety of others;

g) the determination to work through the project from beginning to end;

h) an ability to identify, explore and evaluate different alternatives of technique or approach before proceeding;

i) an ability to assess the progress of the project objectively and to act accordingly.

As with all criteria lists, these nine areas are not intended to constitute a definitive assessment account, any assessment list, grid or method would depend upon the particular requirements of the relevant examining board.

Keeping a Record

The importance of record keeping has been stressed throughout the above example. One straightforward method would be for the pupil to keep a project diary, which not only provides a readily accessible means of referring to previous work, but which also helps to ensure that evidence exists that the pupil has undertaken the set tasks. As with all recording activity it would be the teacher's responsibility to check regularly the entries, which should in turn help the assessment process. Regular diary updates would also go some way towards ensuring that work in progress was the pupil's own unaided work, as well as helping to sustain his or her motivation.

NB Different GCSE Examination Boards prescribe different assessment and record-keeping methods. It is obviously important, therefore, to consult the relevant guidelines before introducing any scheme.

Classroom Management

The project example described above in some detail could have been a brief set by the teacher designed to incorporate previous knowledge and to promote the discovery of new knowledge. If this were the case then it would be appropriate to discuss the implications of the brief with the class before starting work. Such discussions help to clarify in the pupil's mind not only what the project requirements are, but also how those requirements may be translated into textiles. From this point the teacher then assumes the role of negotiator and advisor, and the pupil that of investigator.

Investigation requires access to relevant resources; the textiles teacher is the manager of those resources. Clearly some thought needs to be given how best to organise the textiles room in order to promote an investigatory procedure. The following plan offers one solution.

1 Make sure that all the equipment and materials needed are easily accessible to the class group, i.e. site them sensibly in the room.

2 An informal, yet workshop-like, atmosphere can be quickly created by grouping tables.

3 The nature of investigation often entails various activities taking place simultaneously. The teacher should attempt to classify these different activities (e.g. reading, designing, art and craft, sewing) and create table areas accordingly.

4 Some investigatory activities require more space than others. Spray dyeing, for example, demands self-contained space away from a sewing area but in close proximity to a water supply. The tables used should be protected by covering with newspaper and/or polythene.

5 Where space is limited, the walls can be used for certain activities. Diffusing can be done successfully on a vertical surface. The walls can be protected by newspaper attached by low-tack adhesive tape or fixing agents such as Blu-tack.

6 Shelves make good resource areas, not just for storing books and magazines, but also for design stimuli such as plants, shells, driftwood, rock pieces and so on.

7 Try to create a 'Newsboard', somewhere in the room, which will contain up-to-date information on places of interest like Museums of Costume, Embroidery Exhibitions, Art Galleries etc. Needless to say the walls in the room should also feature examples of work, posters and other visual pieces which all contribute to a stimulating textiles environment.

8 The absence of a sink in the room can be overcome by using bowls and buckets. Water can be successfully stored in polythene bottles and other similar containers.

It should be emphasised, however, that the textiles room is only one resource. It is not realistic or desirable to expect the textiles teacher to anticipate and cater for every aspect of the subject. Pupils are to be encouraged to see the wider implications of textiles as a curriculum area. To this end pupils may well need to seek advice and assistance from the Art department (for design), the History department (for knowledge of social history, period costume) and so on. These links help to promote an understanding of the wider implications of textiles in everyday life, rather than being merely an isolated subject having little or no connection with the world at large.

Glossary of terms

Acetate — Clear plastic film used for overhead projectors.

Adjusted design — A design which has been improved from the original.

Airbrush — A hand-held device, usually slightly larger than a fountain pen, that sprays paint, ink or dye using compressed air. The airbrush gives a fine spray and is used on small areas for detailed work.

Appliqué — Known also as applied work, it is the method of attaching one fabric to another (usually the background fabric) using decorative stitches.

Colourphelt — A non-woven fabric available in many colours, used mainly for craft work as a cheap substitute for felt.

Colour wash — A diluted form of dye or paint used to cover a background, in bands of different colours.

Design transference — The process of copying a design from paper to fabric.

Diffuser — A simple mouth-operated piece of equipment used for spraying paint, ink or dye by blowing (diffusing).

Fabric manipulation — Changing the surface appearance of the fabric by folding, gathering, tearing, fraying etc.

Fabric marker — A blue non-permanent water-based marking pen. Outlines drawn with this pen either fade or can be removed with water.

Flat knot — (Also called the square knot.) Consisting of two half-knots which form the basis of Macramé work.

Flesh out — Add substance to, or develop.

Initial design — The first attempt at producing a finished design from the working drawings.

Isolate — To focus on a particular aspect of something in order to develop this into a design.

Line up — To place in line.

Macramé — An Arabic word. The ancient art of knotting derived from netting and sailors' knots.

Masking out — The process of blocking out or covering (with tape, paper, etc.) that part of a design which is to be left uncoloured when spraying, screening, or stippling.

Mitre — The method of diagonal (45°) seaming to form right-angled corners.

Mounting — The method of presenting finished embroidery by means of stretching and lacing.

Needleweaving — Defined as a modern version of the ancient craft of weaving; it is worked with a needle over warp-threads (attached to fabric, wood, card etc.) to produce an open web-like effect.

Notch cut — Removing a small triangular or wedge-shaped piece of fabric.

Padding — The raising of a defined surface area by the use of wadding.

Padded appliqué — (Also called Appliqué quilting.) The background fabric is slit behind the appliqué shape, the wadding inserted, and the slit oversewn.

Patchwork — Of peasant origin. The result of sewing together geometrically shaped pieces of fabric.

Piped edge — A narrow strip of bias fabric which projects from the edge of an article.

Pipette — A tube which is narrow at one end and bulbous at the other used for transferring fluids.

Prick and pounce — The method of transferring a design to fabric by pricking the traced design with a needle and patting through powdered tailors' chalk.

Quilting — Three layers of material (e.g. fabric, wadding, muslin) stitched together to form a raised design.

Random	Without any set design.
Score	Indenting (but *not* cutting through) the surface of card in order to make crisp folds.
Scrunched	Tightly crumpled or creased.
Shade	A colour with black added.
Soft sculpture	The representation of objects by three-dimensional fabric form.
Spray dyeing	The process of applying dye to a fabric surface using an airbrush, spray gun or diffuser.
Spray gun	A similar device to the airbrush but larger. As the name suggests this device is usually operated by a trigger, and it is capable of spraying large areas with paint, ink or dye.
Stencil	A mask of card from which relevant areas have been cut to reveal those parts of the design to be sprayed, screened or stippled.
Straight of grain	The warp thread of a fabric which runs parallel to the selvedge.
Suffolk puffs	A circle of fabric gathered around the edge and pulled up to form a puff. Derived in Suffolk, each puff is joined together to form a patchwork.
Surface stitchery	An embellishment to the surface of the work.
Template	A piece of robust material (usually card) cut accurately to a desired shape. The template is traced around in order to transfer the outline accurately.
Trace off	The process of copying a drawing or design exactly by using transparent paper.
Trace tacking	A method of transferring a design by marking the design on to the fabric by using running stitches.
Tint	A colour with white added.
Tone	A colour with grey added.

Book List for Further Information

Beaney, Jan. *Stitches: New Approaches*. Batsford. 1985
Brown, Pauline. *Embroidery Backgrounds—Painting and Dyeing Techniques*. Batsford. 1984.
Cave, Oenone. *Traditional Smocks and Smocking*. Mills and Boon. 1979.
Coleman, Anne. *The Creative Sewing Machine*. Batsford. 1979.
Gamble, Margaret. *Creative Textiles: Project Ideas for GCSE*. Edward Arnold 1987.
Robinson, Stuart and Patricia. *Exploring Fabric Printing*. Mills & Boon. 1972.
Schmid-Burleson, Donny. *The Technique of Macramé*. Batsford. 1974.
Littlejohn, Jean. *Fabrics for Embroidery*. Batsford. 1986.
Messent, Jan. *Embroidery and Nature*. Batsford. 1984.
Needlecraft 15 Series—Patchwork 2. Search Press. 1985.
　　　　　—Quilting. Search Press. 1985.

Suppliers

Design, Art and Craft Materials

E. J. Arnold and Son Ltd.,
Parkside Lane,
Dewsbury Road,
Leeds. LS1 5TD.
(Cutting boards, cutters, fabric dyes/paints, acetate,
mouth diffusers, air brushes, spray guns, pipettes)

Dylon International Ltd.,
Lower Sydenham,
London. SE20 5HD.
(Dylon dyes, fabric paints)

Dryad,
P.O. Box 38,
Northgates,
Leicester. LE1 9BU.
(Craft equipment and materials)

Berol Ltd.,
Oldmeadow Road,
King's Lynn,
Norfolk. PE30 4JR.
(Craft equipment, fabric dyes, block printing ink)

Embroidery and Fabrics

W. H. Bennett & Sons Ltd.,
79 Piccadilly,
Manchester. M1 2BN.
(Silk, muslin, plain fabrics)

B. Brown (Holborn) Ltd.,
32–33 Greville Street,
London. EC1N 8TD.
(Felt, imitation suede, PVC, colourphelt)

Ells and Farrier Ltd.,
5, Princes Street,
London. W1.
(Beads)

de Denne Ltd.,
159–161 Kenton Road,
Kenton, Harrow,
Middlesex.
(General embroidery supplies)

Homer Textiles Ltd.,
76 Gringers Lane,
Cradley Heath, Warley,
West Midlands. B64 7BS.
(Courtelle/Polyester Wadding, Calico)

Nottingham Educational Supplies,
17 Ludlow Hill, Melton Road,
West Bridgford, Nottingham. NG2 6HD.
(A large selection of embroidery craft and art equipment
and materials)

60 Plus Textiles,
Barley, Nelson, Lancs.
(Plain cottons, sheetings, patchwork, bales)

Texere Yarns,
9, Peckover Street,
Bradford, West Yorkshire. BD1 5HD.
(Threads and yarns)

Whaleys (Bradford) Ltd.,
Harris Court, Great Horton,
Bradford, West Yorks. BD7 4EQ.
(Cottons ready prepared for dyeing and painting, water
dissolvable fabrics)